WALKING IN PEMBROKESHIRE

About the Authors

As professional outdoor writers and photographers, Dennis and Jan Kelsall have written and illustrated many guides covering some of the country's most popular walking areas, and have a weekly walking column in the Lancashire Evening Post.

Their enjoyment of the countryside extends beyond a love of fresh air and open spaces and an appreciation of scenery. They have a keen interest in the environment, its geology, flora and wildlife as well as a passion for delving into the local history that so often provides a clue to interpreting the landscape.

Dennis and Jan's association with Pembrokeshire began with regular camping holidays as children with their respective families, and has continued in later life as they found themselves increasingly drawn to this beautiful corner of Britain. From walking the coast path and exploring the inland countryside over many years, they have come to regard Pembrokeshire as one of Britain's finest walking areas.

Dennis and Jan Kelsall have written and contributed to walking guides covering many popular areas of the country, including *The Pembrokeshire Coastal Path* and *The Ribble Way*, also published by Cicerone.

WALKING IN PEMBROKESHIRE

by

Dennis and Jan Kelsall

2 POLICE SQUARE, MILNTHORPE, CUMBRIA LA7 7PY
www.cicerone.co.uk

© Dennis and Jan Kelsall 2005
First published 2005
Reprinted 2008
ISBN-13: 978 1 85284 431 8
ISBN-10: 1 85284 431 0

British Library Cataloguing-in-Publication Data
A catalogue record for this book is available from the British Library
Photos by the authors

Acknowledgements

Pembrokeshire is distinct within Wales. It has its own special qualities and has hung on to the 'separateness' of its identity despite the bureaucratic urge for conglomeration over recent decades. This is a reflection of the passion emanated by its people for the county, and barely a walk went by when we did not meet somebody quietly eager to impart their local knowledge, point out secluded corners or the best place for a view, and relate tales of local happenings that never appear in the history books.

Such enthusiasm is infectious, and greatly added to our enjoyment in undertaking this project. Although too numerous to mention individually – even if we did know all their names – we would like to express our thanks to everyone who offered us help in one way or another, from the benefit of their knowledge to a welcome cup of tea on a hot afternoon (and even getting us back on the road the same day when our vehicle needed repair). We would also like to thank the staff of the National Park and the County Council for their advice and practical assistance, and for the work they have done in making the countryside and coast accessible.

Front cover: Musselwick Sands (Walk 8)

CONTENTS

Part IV – Rivers, woodland and a lake

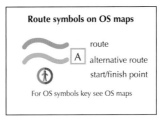

Route symbols on OS maps

route

A alternative route

start/finish point

For OS symbols key see OS maps

Advice to Readers

Readers are advised that while every effort is taken by the authors to ensure the accuracy of this guidebook, changes can occur which may affect the contents. It is advisable to check locally on transport, accommodation, shops, etc, but even rights of way can be altered.

The publisher would welcome notes of any such changes.

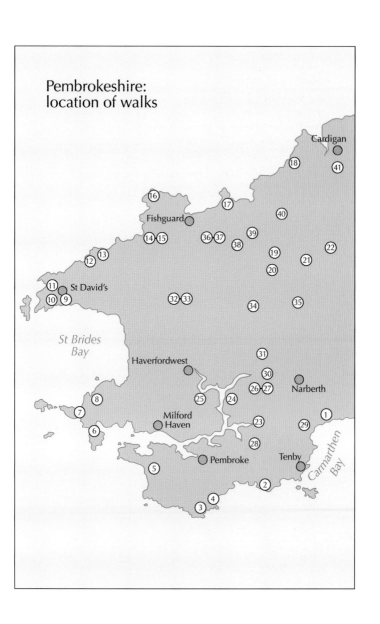

Pembrokeshire:
location of walks

Cardigan

Fishguard

St David's

St Brides
Bay

Haverfordwest

Milford
Haven

Narberth

Pembroke

Tenby

Carmarthen
Bay

Along the old tramway in Pleasant Valley (Walk 1)

INTRODUCTION

Like the Finisterre of Galicia and the Land's End of England, Pembrokeshire (or Pen-fro) has the same meaning for the Welsh, 'the end of the land'. The southwesternmost tip of Wales, it presents a similar outline to the open seas as its more southerly namesakes, with ragged peninsulas reaching out towards the setting sun. Settled in the earliest times, these drawn-out strips of habitation share other things too: the roots of their Celtic culture, vividly portrayed in the enigmatic remains of ancient settlements and sacred sites; the commonality of native language; a passion for storytelling, legend and song. It is a place of great dramatic beauty, where land and sea stand in hoary confrontation, with bastions of craggy cliffs pushed back behind sweeping bays, and innumerable tiny coves separated by defiant promontories. But not everywhere is the demarcation clear. Tidal estuaries and twisting rivers penetrate deep into the heartland, where steep-sided valleys and sloping woodlands climb to a gently undulating plateau. The countryside is chequered with a myriad of small fields and enclosures bound by herb-rich boundaries of stone, earth and hedge. Even higher ground rises in the north, not true mountains perhaps in the expected sense, but bold, rolling, moorland hills from whose detached elevations the panorama extends far beyond the confines of the county's borders.

THE LEGACY OF THE PAST

There are few large towns, yet Pembrokeshire proudly boasts a city, the smallest in the land, which grew around the memory of Wales' patron saint, David. It is a landscape of small villages and settlements, many at first sight quite deceiving of their past importance. But evidence of their history can often still be found, in the form of ancient churches, ruined castles, crumbling piers and the relics of industry, as well as the sometimes less tangible but equally voluble clues in prehistoric earthworks, enigmatic stones and even the very names of places and features. That collective story paints a very different picture to that seen today, in which Pembrokeshire appears remote from the cores of industry, commerce and administration, unconnected by motorways or air terminals, and with few main roads.

Up until the beginning of the last century, Pembrokeshire was less 'land's end' and more 'gateway', not on the periphery but rather at the hub. Before the coming of the railways it was a maritime land, the focus of a

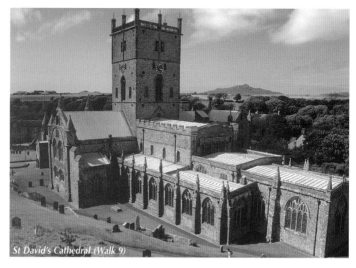

St David's Cathedral (Walk 9)

web of sea routes to Britain's great ports, Ireland, northwest Europe and beyond. Despite the dangers and vagaries of sea, weather and navigation, travel by boat around the coasts was relatively commonplace, and for bulky or weighty cargoes was the only economically practical means of transport. Five thousand years ago there was trade with Ireland, bringing precious gold and copper from the Wicklow Mountains to the main centres of Bronze Age civilisation in southern Britain on Salisbury Plain. For the Celts too, the sea was a highway, encouraging migration, the spread of ideas and the exchange of artefacts and produce. After the Romans left this island, Christendom established itself along the very same routes and Pembrokeshire assumed an

importance comparable with other notable devotional centres around Britain such as Iona off Mull, and Holy Island on the Northumberland coast. It was from here in AD432 that St Patrick set sail to unify Christianity in Ireland, and during the early centuries of the second millennium two or three pilgrimages to St David's had the same spiritual standing as a journey to Rome or Jerusalem. The Vikings were less welcome visitors, but the Welsh never lost the thread of their independent culture, even with the later settlement in at least part of Pembrokeshire by the Normans. Important trading ports developed throughout the medieval period such as Tenby and Pembroke, under the protection of great castles that sought both to establish authority over the land and define a frontier line of defence. Political quarrels with Spain and, later, France saw the strengthening of fortifications, most spectacularly around the vast inlet of The Haven, where naval dockyards exploited one of the world's finest natural harbours, and which Nelson considered second only to Trincomalee in present-day Sri Lanka.

Bringing a previously unimaginable speed and ease to land travel in the 1840s, the early railways found in Pembrokeshire the quickest route from London to the western seaboard. They created a link from the first landfall with suitable harbour facilities for Irish and transatlantic shipping, whereby passengers and mail could reach London in the shortest possible time. Under the engineering genius of Brunel, new ports were built at Neyland and Fishguard. The hoped-for prosperity was short-lived, an economic disappointment repeated during the latter part of the 20th century when the oil and power industry's ambitions for the development of The Haven declined.

THE NATIONAL PARK

Today quiet and unhurried, Pembrokeshire is largely uncrowded by either residents or visitors, and has been spared much of the adverse consequence of the urban and industrial developments of recent decades. The unspoiled magnificence of its coastline, almost 200 miles (320km) of cliffs, bays, beaches and inlets, was recognised in its unique designation as a coastal National Park in 1952. Only the industrial areas lining the higher reaches of The Haven, and a short stretch abutting the Irish ferry terminal at Fishguard, were excepted. Many of Pembrokeshire's other areas of outstanding beauty and important natural habitat were incorporated too: the Preseli Hills, the Gwaun Valley and the tidal reaches of the Daugleddau. But outside the park boundaries the countryside is not to be ignored, for there is an abundance of natural woodland, hidden valleys and pleasant riverside to explore.

PEMBROKESHIRE'S COAST

For the rambler, Pembrokeshire is nothing short of pure delight. Long-distance walkers will already know it for its 180-mile (290km) Coastal Footpath, arguably one of the finest routes in Britain. But its ready accessibility and serpentine geography ideally suit it for those with more modest ambitions too, and many of the most beautiful and dramatic sections provide splendid part- or full-day excursions. From a gentle 2-mile stroll to more challenging 12-mile hike, there is something for everyone in walks that follow the tops of precipitous cliffs or delve into secluded sandy coves. Examples of just about every type of coastal

Scrub cloaks the cliffs behind Castlebeach Bay (Walk 6)

feature are explored, from cavernous blowholes to natural bridges, from solitary stacks to evidence of glacial erosion. Indeed, almost the whole geological history of the coast is revealed from the very earliest pre-Cambrian rocks exposed around St David's to the sand dunes and shingle banks still in the process of being created today.

For the most part undisturbed by large settlement, wildlife of one kind or another is an ever-present distraction. Wildflowers carpet the coastal fringe, and animals such as foxes and rabbits are commonplace. There are plenty of other small mammals too, whilst adders and lizards can occasionally be found sunning themselves on the rocks. These are food for the many predatory birds that patrol the cliffs; kestrels and buzzards hover and wheel in the sky, and the peregrine falcon is once again nesting at a few sites along the coast. Chough and raven are everywhere, as is the ubiquitous pigeon, but it is the seabirds that understandably command the greatest attention. In spring and early summer during the breeding and feeding season, inaccessible cliffs around the coast – as well as the offshore islands such as Ramsey, Skomer, Skokholm and Grassholm – attract countless birds. Umpteen species, both resident and visiting, can be seen, and include gannet, fulmar, Manx shearwater, storm petrel, shag, cormorant, kittiwake, tern, guillemot, puffin and, of course,

the razorbill, which the National Park has adopted as its emblem. The cliffs are a superb vantage for watching Atlantic grey seals, which appear at many places along Pembrokeshire's coast throughout the year. They are most numerous during late spring and early autumn, when large numbers arrive to give birth to their pups. The rocky heads of tiny isolated coves or the dark recesses of sea caves serve as nurseries, which echo to the melancholy cries of the white pups awaiting their mothers' return. You might also see some of the less-common visitors such as porpoises or dolphins and, if you are really lucky, perhaps a minke or orca whale.

Porth Ffynnon (Walk 9)

Rock folding beside the Daugleddau (Walk 24)

AN UNSPOILT HINTERLAND

Away from the coast the walking is equally fine and there is just as much to see. Bold in profile and totally unspoilt, the Preseli Hills impart a wonderful sense of remoteness. Yet they are easily reached and on a fine day offer relaxed walking that is hard to beat. The views extend from one end of Wales to the other, and the mountains of Ireland are visible across the sea. Although lacking the rugged summits of Snowdonia or the English Lakeland hills, the tops are broken by enigmatic craggy outcrops, jumbled heaps of fractured rock that when half hidden by tendrils of swirling mist would not appear out of place in some alien planetary landscape. More mystery and conjecture is evoked by the numerous burial mounds, earth-works and cairns that litter the slopes, vestiges of civilisations that spanned 3000 years, from the time when the pyramids were built in Egypt until the Romans arrived in Britain in AD43.

Less well known – but just as fas-cinating – the tidal reaches of the Daugleddau have their own special magic. An abundance of birdlife is attracted by the rich mudflats exposed at low water, with many birds arriving to overwinter in the relative shelter of the estuary. Ancient oak woods cloak the valley slopes and harbour a lavish variety of flowers almost throughout the year. Often deserted today, the woodland conceals clues to the indus-trial and social history of the settlements that sprang up along the river's banks. The waterway once teemed with barges and small boats, a trading route from the heart of the county to the open sea. But the area was busy in its own right too, for just below the surface are extensive coal-fields that were exploited from as early as the 16th century. Many of the seams are of high-quality anthracite that was exported as far afield as Singapore, but although the industry persisted into the last century there is hardly any trace left today. Overgrown dells and abandoned trackways, or rotting piers backed by a handful of cottages, are now almost the only visible evidence of a once thriving community.

Above the tidal limit, Pembrokeshire's rivers run fast and clear, often through narrow gorges where man's only exploitation has been to manage the centuries-old woodland cloaking the steep slopes. With a wealth of native species such as birch, ash, holly and oak, their continuity has been preserved by coppicing, selective felling and natural regeneration. Relatively undis-turbed by human activity and providing shelter and food, these are havens for all manner of wildlife. Blackbird, wren, chiffchaff, nuthatch, chaffinch, goldfinch, blue and great tits, and green and spotted wood-peckers are just some of the birds you might see. Squirrels and small rodents scurry about and foxes and badgers are fairly common, although you need to be there at dusk to catch sight of Mr Brock. Ancient woodland is to be

15

The Coast Path at Freshwater West (Walk 5)

found elsewhere too, perhaps most notably in the north at Pentre Evan and Tycanol, noted for the ferns and lichens that grow in abundance amongst the hillside boulders and upon the trunks of the trees. Although rivers and streams are plentiful, there are no significant natural lakes in the county. However, since its opening in 1972 the Llys-y-frân Reservoir has established itself as a splendid substitute, attracting an ever-growing diversity of wildlife as well as providing a fine recreational facility and meeting the water supply needs of the area.

One of the great delights in wandering through Pembrokeshire is to savour its quiet, narrow lanes. The herbal splendour found along the cliff path and in the woods is repeated

here and the banks and hedges are packed with interest throughout the year. Bramble, gorse, heather, hazel, blackthorn and honeysuckle abound, and there is an almost continuous succession of flowers sprouting from the crevices and beneath the bushes. Violet, primrose, lesser celandine, bluebell, campion, wood anemone, herb robert, foxglove, tormentil, stitchwort and the ever-present parsleys; the list is almost endless.

A FEW PRACTICALITIES

Whether following the coast, wandering the hills or exploring the valleys and woods, the walking everywhere is superb and will invariably reveal something unexpected along the way. Unless you really are an expert it is a good idea to take along pocket flower and bird field guides, and a small pair of binoculars will prove invaluable, especially along the coast. Pembrokeshire's roads are generally quiet and parking is rarely a problem, but where there is no formal car park, please ensure your vehicle is not causing an obstruction. All the main access points along the coast are served by excellent bus services, and plans are being made to extend these into the Preseli Hills and possibly the Gwaun Valley. The walks described in this collection are all circular, but local transport offers the possibility of turning some of them into shorter one-way routes. Please use the buses where you can, as this will help sustain the case for further improvements and keep the lanes enjoyable for walkers, cyclists and horse riders. Timetables and information are available at local Tourist Information Centres and from the Greenways website (see the information section in the Appendix), but note that some routes operate a reduced service from October until the end of April.

Nowhere is the walking overly demanding, but be aware that, particularly along some sections of the coast, paths can make successive steep climbs and descents, which can be tiring if you are unused to strenuous routes. The Pembrokeshire climate is generally mild, and even the middle of winter can produce delightful days when the shining sun warms the air. But snow does lie from time to time on the Preseli Hills, and mist and cloud can cause navigational difficulties there for the inexperienced. Wind and rain may occur at any time, but providing you are equipped with suitable weatherproof clothing need not spoil your enjoyment. However, take care, especially along the cliffs, which are sometimes slippery underfoot and where unexpected gusts can force you off balance. Walking boots offer the best protection for your ankles on rough ground, and gaiters help to keep your feet dry. As with all country walking, paths may be muddy during and after wet weather, and lush summer vegetation often makes trousers more appropriate than shorts.

Past Maiden Castle to Great Treffgarne Rocks (Walk 32)

The bank of the Eastern Cleddau by Tal-y-bont Wood (Walk 31)

On some of the walks you need to be aware of how the tide will run during the course of the day. Beaches may have coves that are cut off as the tide rises, and if you venture down you need to keep an eye open as the water comes in. However, three walks exploring the upper reaches of the Daugleddau are affected too: from Cresswell Quay, Landshipping Quay and Little Milford Wood. Details of the sections affected are given within the appropriate chapters, and you can get information on tide times from local Tourist Information Centres or by consulting the National Park's free newspaper Coast to Coast.

Recent years have seen an increase in the resources applied to the maintenance of the county's footpath network and rangers from both Pembrokeshire's National Park and County Council have done much to improve the paths in the area. New bridges, stiles and gates have been installed and many routes have been reopened after becoming almost lost, whilst ongoing maintenance work includes cutting back vegetation growth. Inevitably problems will be encountered from time to time and the authorities welcome information that helps them keep on top of these. Contact details are given in the Appendix.

Part I

Walks along the Coast

Cliff erosion leaves spectacular stacks (Walk 4)

WALK 1
Amroth and Pleasant Valley

Start	Amroth (SN162071)
Distance	4.5 miles (7.2km)
Time	2.25hr
Height gain	800ft (245m)
OS map	Explorer OL36 South Pembrokeshire
Parking	National Park car park by the Amroth Arms
Route features	Paths may be muddy, steepish climbs and descents
Public transport	Bus service to Amroth
Refreshments	Pubs in Amroth and at Wiseman's Bridge, tearoom at Colby Woodland Gardens
Toilets	Amroth and Wiseman's Bridge

This area has not always been the quiet backwater it appears today, for until the beginning of the 20th century heavy industry scarred the landscape with coal mines, brickworks and iron smelters. Now left to its own devices, Nature has draped a soft green veil over the debris of abandonment, a fascinating focus for this splendid walk.

An unassuming little village at the southeast corner of Pembrokeshire's coast, Amroth offers one of the finest holiday beaches in the area. It is also blessed with some beautiful countryside, lush semi-natural woodland that fills the several deep valleys cleaving the hills behind the coast.

Walk from the car park onto the sea front road by the Amroth Arms and turn right. Where the road shortly curves inland by some toilets at the end of the promenade, abandon it for the coast path. It climbs steeply through the trees behind onto the headland, from where there is a splendid view back along the coast.

Over a stile at the top, carry on along the upper edge of a narrow field. Leave through either a kissing gate part-way along, or a stile at the end, to continue along a gravel track that gives onto a lane. Head downhill to Wiseman's Bridge, staying on the lane behind the beach. When it swings away at the far end, leave beside a stream, following a path past a toilet block into the lush woodland of Pleasant Valley.

THE COAST PATH

One of Pembrokeshire's finest assets is the 180-mile (290km) long-distance path that traces its entire coastal fringe, and every year heavily loaded walkers are to be seen embarking from or arriving at Amroth, its southern terminus. There is a plaque commemorating the official opening in 1970 by Wynford Vaughn Thomas at the eastern end of the promenade next to a bridge spanning a stream that marks the county boundary. Although it can obviously be accomplished in either direction, starting here offers an infinitely more satisfying experience in the gradual exchange of the softer scenery of Carmarthen Bay for the savage beauties that are characteristic of the northern coast.

The undulating hills behind the coast overlie abundant carboniferous coal deposits, the source of some of the best-quality anthracite to be had in the country. Much folded, the layers of black gold rise close to the surface in places and have been scratched at since the earliest times. The coal was dug from simple 'bell' pits and drift mines, and their collapsed vestiges can still be traced in the innumerable hollows concealed by the dense woodland cover of both Pleasant Valley and Colby Valley. The advent of the industrial age brought large-scale exploitation, and the sea offered an economy and ease of transport to the enterprise, which few inland sources could match. Deep mining for the richest seams began in earnest and horse-drawn tramways, later upgraded with the

21

Wiseman's Beach

development of the steam engine, were laid to carry the coal to ships waiting at nearby Saundersfoot's harbour. The path through Pleasant Valley follows the old tramway that ran to the coast, and if you explore the Coast Path just beyond Wiseman's Bridge you'll pass through the tunnels that took the route beneath the cliffs. By the 19th century, however, the most productive reserves were becoming worked out and what remained proved increasingly difficult to extract because of faulting. Production declined in the face of competition from the South Wales valleys, although because of its high quality some coal was still mined into the beginning of the 20th century.

Briefly rejoin the lane, but then slip back into the trees by Tramway Cottage, continuing along the line of the tramway along which coal and iron from Stepaside's collieries and smelt hearths was transported to ships waiting in Saundersfoot's harbour. Stick to the main path, subsequently crossing the stream and eventually emerging onto another lane.

The local shales also contained abundant iron ore deposits, and during the later part of the 19th century these sustained a burgeoning industry that produced a high-quality pig iron. The proximity of coal suitable for the smelting process and a ready means of transport made the industry highly profitable and supported an ironworks with two blast furnaces. The Stepaside Iron Works, whose ruins stand beside the route as it leaves Pleasant Valley, opened in 1849, and the increased traffic to the harbour at Saundersfoot justified the replacement of the horse-drawn tramway carts by steam engines. Yet, despite its success, the enterprise was relatively short-lived, and little more than 30 years later the furnaces were left to grow cold.

Walk left, but just past the entrance to the former Grove Colliery and Stepaside Iron Works – where the impressive remains of some of the old buildings and ore hoppers can still be seen – turn off into Mill House Caravan Park. Go forward where the drive then curves beyond the ablution block, passing between a couple of

The Stepaside Iron Works

WEALTHY LANDOWNER'S RETREAT

During the 18th and 19th centuries, the coal and iron industries brought considerable employment to the area. They also made a lot of money for the owners, one of whom, John Colby, bought land in the valley behind Amroth in 1787. However, it was not only the mineral wealth that attracted him, for he was also impressed by the natural loveliness of the valley itself, and in the early 19th century began the construction of a mansion, Colby Lodge. Half a century later a Lancashire man, Samuel Kay, bought the estate, and with the help of his plant-collecting brother created a magnificent exotic woodland on the valley slopes around the big house, together with an enchanting walled garden. These have since been given to the National Trust and are open to visitors between spring and autumn.

caravans to a stile at their rear. Bear left up a hillside pasture and leave through a gap in the top wall onto a narrow lane, following it away to the right.

Having crested a low hill, the lane descends to a sharp bend by cottages. Take the track off ahead, but where that subsequently splits, look over to the right for a waymarked stile. The way rises across the shrubby flanks of Staggers Hill, continuing upwards at the edge of the meadows above and shortly joining a hedged track. Where that then turns, go over a stile facing you onto a lesser wood-girt path, walking ahead until you ultimately reach Cwmrath Farm. To the right, its access track leads out to a lane.

Go right, but then almost immediately left onto a bridleway that leads to a farm. Where the track turns into the yard, keep ahead along a narrower waymarked path which, dropping ever more steeply, zigzags into a thickly wooded valley. Stick with the main trail, and, at the bottom walk past a small building and cross a stream to emerge onto a lane.

To the right (after passing the private access to Colby Lodge), turn in at the entrance of Colby Woodland Gardens, which is signed as the Knight's Way to the coast. Beyond the tearoom and ticket office, the track meanders pleasantly along the delightful valley. Eventually reaching cottages, it ends at a lane that leads back down to the car park in Amroth.

WALK 2
Manorbier

Start	Manorbier (SS061975)
Distance	2.5 miles (4km)
Time	1.25hr
Height gain	580ft (175m)
OS map	Explorer OL36 South Pembrokeshire
Parking	Car park by beach below castle (charge)
Route features	Coastal path and field and farm tracks
Public transport	Seasonal bus service to Manorbier
Refreshments	Chives Tea Room and Castle Inn in Manorbier
Toilets	Beside car park at Manorbier

For Giraldus Cambrensis, Manorbier was 'the pleasantest spot in Wales'. Although he might be accused of bias since he was born in the castle, Giraldus had travelled widely throughout the country and across Europe as far as Rome, and must have seen a great many other places against which to set a comparison. His sentiments are not unfounded, and the view across the valley from the elegant church of St James to his one-time home still holds great attraction.

The castle has an imposing location, gazing out over Manorbier's sandy bay, and was founded at the beginning of the 12th century by the Norman knight Odo de Barri. The original fortification would have been of wood protected by earthen ramparts and it was his son, William, who began the stone fortress. Built from the local hard limestone it has survived the passing centuries well and boasts many fine features, including state apartments, a baronial hall and a brutally powerful gatehouse.

Walk through the car park away from the beach to the far right corner and there double back right on a track that

This walk explores the coast to the east of Manorbier, where there is a splendid little cromlech and also some striking examples of unusual cliff erosion, before returning to the village along a quiet inland valley.

GERALD OF WALES

The de Barris held the manor for over 250 years, but it was Odo's youngest grandson, Giraldus Cambrensis – Gerald of Wales – who is most remembered today. Born in 1145, he was a remarkable scholar and, before he died at the age of 77, had written some 17 books. Unlike his brothers who followed military careers, Gerald entered the Benedictine abbey of St Peter in Gloucester when he was 13 and later went to St David's. Although offered bishoprics in Ireland and several places in Wales, his life's ambition was to oversee St David's, but after many rejections Gerald's zeal finally waned and he spent his remaining years writing. He had travelled extensively during his life and his prolific literary legacy provides many amusing anecdotes and fascinating insights into the life of the period, albeit sometimes erring on the fanciful.

Manorbier Castle

climbs the hill above to the church. Walk up through the graveyard and go right at its top edge, continuing along a hedged path signed 'To the Coast Path'. Shortly, the King's Quoit dolmen becomes visible ahead, but instead of falling to it the path climbs again to a junction. Turn right, dropping to meet the Coast Path beside the burial chamber.

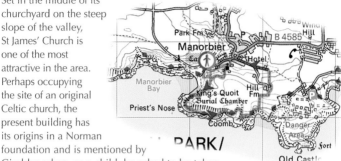

Set in the middle of its churchyard on the steep slope of the valley, St James' Church is one of the most attractive in the area. Perhaps occupying the site of an original Celtic church, the present building has its origins in a Norman foundation and is mentioned by Giraldus when, as a child, he asked to be taken there for safety during a Welsh raid on the Norman stronghold of Tenby in 1153. The oldest part of the church can be seen in the nave, but the chancel and transepts were rebuilt in the middle of the 13th century. The tower, erected around the same time, must have served a defensive role, for its only access is through a door high in the wall from which the ladder could be drawn up after entering. Other points of interest include the effigy of a mailed recumbent knight with crossed legs; arms on his shield show him to be one of the de Barris, the Norman lords who built the castle.

To the left, the Coast Path continues around the Priest's Nose, passing, just beyond, above a dramatically narrow chasm that falls sheer to the sea, so amazingly precise that it could have been cut by a gigantic saw. There is another gash a little further along, but being wider, is less sensational. Around the point, the view ahead is to the bold prominence of Old Castle Head, site of a prehistoric fort, but now occupied as an artillery training school.

The cromlech is known as the King's Quoit, its capstone, the 'quoit', supposedly hurled by some mighty legendary ruler. Archaeologists, however,

27

Looking back along the cliffs to Priest's Nose

tell us that it is of Neolithic origin, the top slab originally being supported by three uprights, but one has collapsed leaving it canted to the ground. More ancient remains lie on nearby Old Castle Head, but unfortunately this is MOD property and there is no public access. The settlement there dates from the Iron Age, with a number of hut circles being identified. However, it is suggested that the vantage continued to be inhabited long after that time and may have been occupied by the Normans before the castle at Manorbier was begun.

The path carries on above a steepening grassy slope that falls to low bare sandstone cliffs overlooking the sea, later tucking in and dipping behind inaccessible coves, which in turn offer an equally dramatic retrospective view as you climb beyond. After gaining height onto a small headland, the over-vertical cliffs turn in around Presipe Bay and the path leads to a stile at the back.

Climb away from the coast at the field edge, continuing over the hill in the next field. At the bottom corner, go right to meet a track and follow it left beside Hill Farm to a gate. However, ignore the gate and go over a stile in front to drop straight across the fields beyond. At the bottom of the third field, leave through a gap onto a track, opposite which, hidden in the scrubby trees, is a limekiln.

The route back to Manorbier lies to the left over a stile, where you join a track away from the cottage beside it. Keep going past another track from Hill Farm, eventually emerging in the village. The tearoom and pub lie just to the right, whilst the lane downhill leads below the castle back to the car park.

WALK 3
Bosherston and the Lily Ponds

Start	Bosherston (SR966947)
Distance	1.75 miles (2.8km)
Time	1hr
Height gain	445ft (135m)
OS map	Explorer OL36 South Pembrokeshire
Parking	National Trust car park behind Bosherston church
Route features	Lakeside paths
Public transport	Seasonal bus service to Bosherston
Refreshments	Ye Olde Worlde Café and St Govan's Inn at Bosherston
Toilets	Adjacent to car park

The Bosherston Lily Ponds are at their best in early summer when the flowers are in full bloom, and are a favourite destination for many visitors to this part of Pembrokeshire.

The walk described from Stackpole – Walk 4 – brings you to this point from across the bridge. If you want to combine the two, turn left and follow the eastern arm up, referring to the instructions given in the next chapter.

Several paths meander through the old Stackpole estate and offer a choice of easy rambles taking in the splendid woodland of the sheltered valleys, spectacular clifftop scenery and some marvellous beaches as well as the lakes themselves. This and the following walk explore some of the best corners and can either be undertaken individually or combined to make a longer day out.

A path drops from the far end of the car park by the toilets into a wood. Keep ahead past a junction and carry on a little further to reach a causeway across the upper end of the western arm of the lakes. The ongoing path follows the opposite bank, and where the track shortly forks, either way will do (the one on the right crests a rocky prominence from which there is a splendid view across the foot of the three lakes). The ways combine and lead to a second causeway, this crossing the middle arm. Go right on the far side, signed towards Broad Haven, the path winding around to a bridge across the longer, eastern arm. ◄

The Lily Ponds comprise a trio of narrow lagoon-like inlets weaving their watery fingers

Looking up the western arm

inland amidst gently rolling countryside. They are man-made, and were created in the late 18th century by damming the valley behind the beach at Broad Haven to provide a decorative feature for the grand, but now demolished, house of Stackpole Court. Flowering in June, the water lilies thrive on the lime-rich waters, which support an abundance of interesting wildlife. Amongst the birds commonly seen are kingfishers and herons, and the swans that live here often create a splendid show as they take off or land on the water. Equally eye-catching are the iridescent dashes of dragonflies and damselflies. If you walk quietly you might spot large pike lurking in the shady waters by

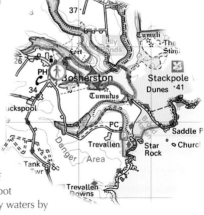

31

Looking from the prehistoric fort

the bank or, if you are very lucky, even see otters splashing about as they hunt for fish.

To return to Bosherston, cross the bridge and follow the path towards Broad Haven. At a junction by the foot of the lake, go right again past the access to Broad Haven beach, cross a small stone bridge and continue up beside the western lake. Later, over a bridge spanning a side creek, walk right, shortly passing an abandoned brick building, an old pump house. At a junction just beyond, go left back up to the car park.

Above the car park and standing on the site of an even earlier building is the charming Norman church of St Michael and All Angels. Inside, under the northern transept window lies a carved tomb, thought to be the Dowager Duchess of Buckingham, whilst on the south side is that of a 14th-century crusader knight. The font is perhaps as old as the church, but many other ancient features were lost during restoration work in the middle of the 19th century.

WALK 4
Stackpole and the Lily Ponds

Start	Stackpole Quay (SR991958)
Distance	5 miles (8km)
Time	2.25hr
Height gain	760ft (230m)
OS map	Explorer OL36 South Pembrokeshire
Parking	National Trust car park above Stackpole Quay
Route features	Coastal, woodland and field paths
Public transport	Seasonal bus service to Stackpole Quay
Refreshments	National Trust tearoom at Stackpole Quay
Toilets	Beside tearoom at Stackpole Quay

From the car park entrance, walk down behind the tearoom and bear right to find a stepped path through a break in the wall, signed to Barafundle. It climbs onto the headland above Stackpole Quay, from where there is a splendid view back east the coast to Caldy Island.

The second of the two walks around the Stackpole estate, this explores the particularly outstanding stretch of limestone cliffs between the old harbour at Stackpole Quay and Broad Haven beach. It then follows the eastern reach of the ornamental ponds before crossing the fields behind the headland to complete the circuit.

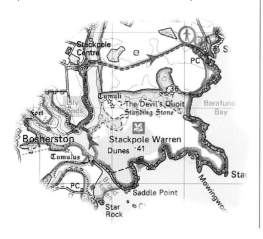

THE STACKPOLE ESTATE

That the Vikings visited the area is suggested by its name, derived from the Norse words stac and pollr, describing an inlet beside an isolated rock, which lies provocatively off the beach. The history of settlement, however, begins in the 13th century when Elidur de Stackpole built a castle here. By the 17th century the estate was in the hands of the Lort family, passing by marriage to the Campbells of Cawdor from Scotland. It was they who built Stackpole Court in 1735, which overlooked the eastern valley for almost 200 years. However, by 1963 the great house had become uninhabitable and was pulled down by the fifth Earl of Cawdor, leaving only the stables standing. He bequeathed a large part of the estate to the National Trust on his death in 1970. The sturdy harbour was built at the end of the 18th century and used to land coal for the estate as well as providing a berth for Lord Cawdor's pleasure yacht, the Speedwich.

Be very careful along this stretch of coast, particularly if it is windy or wet, or there are young children in the party, for the cliffs are precipitous. Remember also that there is no safe pedestrian access to the shore other than at Barafundle and Broad Haven beaches.

An obvious path leads away across a gently undulating limestone plateau, but with all the interest lying in the cliffs below, you will be drawn to investigate every indentation and protrusion of the coast. ◄

The clifftop scenery is quite breathtaking, with spectacular blowholes, fissures and sea caves piercing the cliffs that drop 100ft (30m) sheer to the sea. The coastal walk must have been a particular favourite of the Lort family, for their name is preserved in some of its outstanding features: Lorts Cave and Griffith Lorts Hole.

An arched stone gateway above Barafundle marks the top of a staircase down to the lovely beach, a legacy of the Cawdors' presence. Walk across the sand and climb away at the far side through a copse of sycamore trees. Follow the coast out to Stackpole Head, doubling back past Mowingword and around the spectacular bay beyond, which is littered with huge boulders and stacks displaying every stage of disintegration. The cliffs here attract rock climbers, who scramble up and down with deceptive ease, the crashing waves below giving the

Stackpole Head

The rugged beach below Mowingword

challenging climbs an added exhilaration. The path winds on overlooking more impressive coves, and passing the massive depression of a blowhole. Eventually rounding Saddle Point, the way sweeps in above Broad Haven beach and leaves the close-cropped swathe of the headland through a kissing gate. Turn right towards scrubby sandhills, and climb parallel to a low stone wall running to the left that has become partly engulfed by the shifting sand. Over the crest, bear left and drop through the dunes to reach a path at the bottom.

You now have the choice of returning to Stackpole or making a detour around Bosherston Lily Ponds to the village, where there is a café and pub. ◄

Detour For Bosherston, go left to the head of Broad Haven beach, bear right over a small stone bridge and continue with the instructions given in Walk 3.

For Stackpole, turn right and follow the lake up to a bridge across the foot of the eastern arm. Cross and follow the lakeside to the right, shortly arriving at Eight Arch Bridge. On the far bank, a broad farm track heads away across the fields over a low hill. Ignore crossing tracks and you will eventually return to the car park at Stackpole Quay.

WALK 5
The Angle Peninsula

Start	Freshwater West (SM884004)
Distance	9.75 miles (15.7km)
Time	5hr
Height gain	1625ft (495m)
OS map	Explorer OL36 South Pembrokeshire
Parking	Car park above northern end of Freshwater beach
Route features	Quiet lanes and coastal path; the return is rugged and steeply undulating
Public transport	Seasonal bus service to Freshwater West and Angle
Refreshments	The Point House (pub and restaurant) at Angle and café at West Angle Bay
Toilets	At West Angle Bay

The first half of this walk is relatively undemanding and follows the coast around the shallow inlet of Angle Bay and on through woodland fringe to Angle Point. The return, however, is fairly strenuous, the cliff path being forced abruptly up and down to negotiate clefts where water run-offs fall to the sea. That said, it is a splendid ramble, and on a fine day there are spectacular views all along the cliffs.

A waymarked path leaves the back of the car park across an undulating sea of grassy sandhills. Just before reaching the beach, swing right, the path shortly rising amongst gorse and bracken above the sandstone cliffs closing the northern end of the long strand of Freshwater West. Over a rise, the way drops steeply into a small valley, where you should abandon the Coast Path by using a stile on the right. Towards the top of the gully mount another stile on the left, and walk directly across the fields to reach a lane.

The tide appears lethargic in Angle Bay, the water imperceptibly creeping in and out under

A walk of stark contrast, setting the sheltered inland-facing coast of Milford Haven against the battered high cliffs that present a shoulder to the full force of the Atlantic weather.

Angle Bay

its heavenly influence. At low water extensive mudflats are exposed, rich in worms and burrowing shellfish, and such an abundance of food attracts a wide assortment of birdlife, particularly in winter. Common are oystercatchers, curlews, sandpipers and redshanks, but you'll also see divers, cormorants and, of course, the ubiquitous duck.

Thorn

Rat Island

Castles Ba

Sheep Island

Go left, and then at a junction right down a narrow leafy lane, which curves in front of wrought-iron gates at the bottom to end on the shore. A track to the left leads around Angle Bay, joining a road at its end into the village. Just before reaching the church, turn right onto a pot-holed lane, cross a stream and go right again, continuing around the bay to Point House. Over a stile ahead, follow the edge of successive fields to Angle Point, where a narrow, stepped path hidden in the hedge drops to a stony beach below.

The battered walls are remains of The Haven's first lifeboat station. Established in 1868, it continued in service until 1927, when another boathouse was built a little further along the coast. That too has been superseded by the present station, which was constructed beside it and opened in 1992.

Back in the field, stride on around the point, the way becoming a hedged path and shortly meeting a crossing track (which leads to the modern lifeboat station). Walk forward to a stile at the far side and continue above the coast, again at the perimeter of successive fields.

There is a good view from the path of the oil terminal jetties that march on stilts from the bank to the deepwater channel. The boom years of the 1960s and early 1970s saw the establishment of

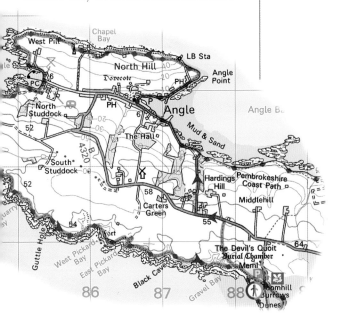

five separate refinery and storage installations along The Haven. However, changing political and economic fortunes lessened the demand for its oil, and instead of the promised continued development there have been large-scale closures, which have inevitably taken their toll upon the local economy. The industrialisation was always a mixed blessing, for although it brought much-needed employment to the area, the risks to the environment have always been high, and when accidents occur they inevitably carry massive and far-reaching implications.

There is soon a view ahead to the Dale peninsula before the path dips into the upper edge of a sycamore wood that falls to the sea below. Hidden in the trees at the far end are gun trenches, part of the outlying fortifications of Chapel Bay Fort, which lies just ahead. Emerging at the far side, join a field track to the right and walk past a couple of cottages to a junction by the entrance to Chapel Bay Fort.

Milford Haven was one of the most heavily defended places in the country during the period of Napoleon's expansionist ambitions. Garrisoned forts and artillery batteries covered the entrance to the waterway and lined both shores as far as Pembroke Dock (where the naval dockyards were situated) and there was even a fort built upon Stack Rock, which lies plumb in the middle of the channel. This walk passes three of the installations: Chapel Bay Fort, currently being restored as a museum; Thorn Island just off the point ahead; and East Block House a little further round, where the massive gun emplacements are largely overgrown with bramble.

Carry on over the stile in front, winding past Chapel Bay Fort and on towards the point. Thorn Island – where the fortifications have been run as a hotel for several

The stretch of cliffs to Rat Island

years – soon comes into view, a narrow stretch of water separating it from the mainland. Rounding the point, the way loses height along craggy cliffs, below which impressive rock folding and erosion is exposed by the tide. Carry on to the head of West Angle beach.

> The gaunt tower rising near the café is all that remains of a brickworks that operated during the latter part of the 19th century, with three kilns producing a range of bricks, tiles and pipes. A narrow band of limestone runs through Angle, which was extensively quarried, the stone being used in the construction of the forts and the naval yards at Pembroke Dock as well as being burnt for agricultural purposes.

Leave at the far side, passing between the café and toilets to a stile. Follow the field edge away above the bay, and after delving through scrub higher up join a track past a disused building, part of a former military installation. The Coast Path then bears right in front of the derelict gun emplacements of the East Block House hidden beneath an overgrowth of bramble, whilst over to the right is the ruin of a Tudor fortification overlooking Rat Island.

Regaining the cliff edge there follows a long, spectacular walk to Freshwater. Striking chasms, sheer-sided coves and natural arches follow in eye-catching succession, each seemingly more wonderful than the last, whilst part-way along is an awesome crater into which the sea washes through a cave. The work of man is seen here too in a couple of promontory forts, one above Sheep Island and another overlooking West Pickard Bay. There is also an unusual octagonal tower, a lookout or lighthouse built above the cliffs. Inevitably, the rugged nature of the coast is reflected in the path, and the walk is demanding with several steep descents and subsequent climbs. However, eventually you meet your outward path above the northern cliffs of Freshwater West and it is not then far back to the car park.

WALK 6
The Dale Peninsula

Start	Dale (SM811058)
Distance	6.5 miles (10.5km)
Time	3.25hr
Height gain	1085ft (330m)
OS map	Explorer OL36 South Pembrokeshire
Parking	Car park at Dale
Route features	Coastal path
Public transport	Seasonal bus service to Dale
Refreshments	Boat House Café and Griffin Inn at Dale
Toilets	By car park at Dale

The path around St Ann's Head, south of Dale, follows a long, convoluted stretch of coast, with constantly changing views as it turns from The Haven towards the open sea. The way back is across a narrow neck of sunken ground, a trench cut by meltwater released at the end of the ice age.

Follow the promenade down to the village, keeping left past the Griffin Inn to leave along a wooded lane rising along the coast towards the field studies centre. When the trees clear towards the far end, look for the Coast Path leaving over a stile on the right. It follows the line of a prehistoric ditch and bank that defended a settlement on the point. Further back lie 19th-century defences, another ditch and wall to protect the landward side of a gun fort, one of several built under Prime Minister Palmerston. It now houses a field studies centre.

The Dale peninsula guards the entrance to Milford Haven and, with its counterpart across the channel – the Angle peninsula – has played an important strategic defensive role throughout history.

The fort is part of a complex series of defences built around the middle of the 19th century in anticipation of an invasion attempt by Napoleon. At first sight it might seem that there was little need for such a show of force, with 15 separate forts and gun

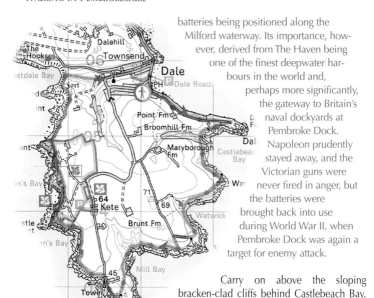

batteries being positioned along the Milford waterway. Its importance, however, derived from The Haven being one of the finest deepwater harbours in the world and, perhaps more significantly, the gateway to Britain's naval dockyards at Pembroke Dock. Napoleon prudently stayed away, and the Victorian guns were never fired in anger, but the batteries were brought back into use during World War II, when Pembroke Dock was again a target for enemy attack.

Carry on above the sloping bracken-clad cliffs behind Castlebeach Bay, the path shortly dropping into one of the several deep-cleft valleys that drain the headland. As you climb away at the far side of the stony beach, look for a limekiln almost hidden beneath the undergrowth. Over a stile follow the field boundary to a second stile where, returning to the scrub above the cliffs, the onward path winds below Watwick Beacon.

The deepwater channel of The Haven made it an ideal harbour to receive the increasingly massive oil tankers that were being developed during the 1960s. During its industrial heyday several terminals, oil refineries and an overland pipeline to Esso's main refinery at Llandarcy were built, as well as an oil-fired power station. However, the approach to the narrow estuary is difficult, and for colossal craft – that might take over a mile to stop – through passage requires both skill and accurate navigation. The soaring beacons on Watwick and

West Blockhouse Points help guide vessels into the inlet, but they failed to prevent the area's worst shipping disaster when, in February 1996, the tanker Sea Empress ran aground, spilling 72,000 tonnes of crude oil into the sea.

Following the field perimeter beyond, watch for a stile back to the cliffs behind Watwick Bay. The main path dips only gently above its head, but a lower path descends to a small beach, exposed at low water. Further on, at West Blockhouse Point, the path passes behind another of Palmerston's forts, this one now owned by the Landmark Trust and available for rent as a holiday cottage with a difference. Beside it stand a trio of navigation markers, whilst to the right of the ongoing path are the concrete wells of the Napoleonic gun emplacements.

The view in front is now to St Ann's Head, on which stands a row of cottages built to accommodate the staff manning the station, a walled vegetable garden, and three lighthouses that at various times have blinked their warnings to passing mariners. Rounding the head of Mill Bay, the path once more dips to the sea, passing the ruined walls of an old mill, fed from a pond formed by damming the stream above.

Castlebeach Bay provides a sheltered mooring

HENRY TUDOR

After 14 years in exile in Brittany, Henry Tudor landed at Mill Bay on 7 August 1485 with a small band of followers. Marching to England, he gathered supporters for his cause along the way and only two weeks later defeated the armies of Richard III at Bosworth Field. Crowned Henry VII, he founded the Tudor dynasty, which would last until the death of Elizabeth I in 1603.

Climb away beyond, working your way round at the field edge to St Ann's Head. Over a stile below the cottages pass the walled garden and continue across open grassland towards the buildings overlooking the point, then follow the boundary fence right to a kissing gate. However, before following the track away from the station, take the cul-de-sac path opposite, which overlooks Cobblers Hole, a particularly striking example of double folding in the strata of the cliffs.

Always a prominent landmark for mariners, St Ann's Head was once the site of a chapel, said to have been built by Henry Tudor in gratitude for his safe landfall. The first official warning beacon here was coal-fired and erected in the mid 17th century. But it did not operate for long, and it was 1714 before a formal light was installed. Two lighthouses were built, which could be aligned to determine position at sea. The rear light was subsequently converted into the coastguard station, whilst the other was re-sited further from the cliff in 1841 because of erosion, and still provides a mark for shipping. When the lights were eventually converted to automatic operation, St Ann's became the control centre for all the installations along the Pembrokeshire coast, with a helicopter pad being added for use by the servicing crew.

Leaving along the driveway, return to the coast through a kissing gate and continue above the cliffs. Now exposed to the full fury of winter gales, the lack of lush vegetation on this side of the headland is a sharp contrast to that facing Milford Haven. Nevertheless, spring sees the bare grass and earthen wall banks burst into colour with hardy clifftop flowers such as spring squill, sea campion and thrift growing so profusely as to form a carpet in places.

The walking is now easy, with dramatic views along the rugged sandstone cliffs, littered with boulders and shattered rocks at their feet. Further on, traces of broken bricks and rubble are relics of HMS Harrier. Formerly a wartime establishment, it continued as a radar and meteorological training school until closure in 1960. Beyond, the path eventually drops to low sandy cliffs behind Westdale Bay that block the western end of a glacial meltwater valley that almost severs the Dale peninsula from the rest of Pembrokeshire. Facing directly towards the Atlantic, a succession of fine waves often roll against the beach, attracting surfers as well as families who just come to enjoy the sand.

Cross a stile at the base of the dip, and strike away over the field. Leave at the far corner, joining a track from Hayguard Hay Farm that leads out to the lane. Keep ahead past the tall-towered church dedicated to St James the Great, but after the houses end turn off right on a track over a cattle grid back to the car park.

A gun emplacement above the West Blockhouse

47

WALK 7
Marloes Sands and the Deer Park

Start	Runwayskiln (SM779081)
Distance	6.5 miles (10.5km)
Time	3.25hr
Height gain	1000ft (305m)
OS map	Explorer OL36 South Pembrokeshire
Parking	National Trust car park by Runwayskiln Youth Hostel
Route features	Coastal path
Public transport	Seasonal bus service to Martin's Haven
Refreshments	Soft drinks at Martin's Haven, and Hook Farm serves tea and coffee
Toilets	At Martin's Haven

With such an extensive unspoilt coastline, it is hardly surprising that there are many splendid beaches to be found in Pembrokeshire. This walk takes you past some of the best, made even more attractive because, although readily accessible, they are often quite empty of people.

The sands along this stretch of coast are backed by spectacular runs of cliff that offer fine views to the offshore islands, and in spring and early summer are a splendid vantage from which to watch the thousands of seabirds that come to breed in the area. From spring until early autumn boat trips leave the tiny cove at Martin's Haven, and – if you can drag yourself away from walking for the day – offer an unforgettable experience.

Leave the car park by the entrance near the Youth Hostel, following the lane away left, signed to the beach. After about 60yd turn off right onto a bridleway, a narrow track squeezed between flower-rich banks that eventually drops to Marloes Sands along a shallow, overgrown gully. On a glorious day you might be tempted to go no further, but the cliffs to the west have an equal attraction. The onward route follows the Coast Path to the right, marked just before you reach the beach.

Near-vertical slabs of striated grey slate lie below the path, becoming more broken as you advance, but as you approach Gateholm you will notice that the island is composed of old red sandstone, an entirely different rock. Erosion has exploited the weaker interface between these two, and although almost separate from the mainland, Gateholm is as yet only an island at high tide.

Gateholm was inhabited during the middle centuries of the first millennium and a complex of around 130 small cells arranged in rows around a rectangular courtyard has been identified. The layout suggests an early monastic settlement, but archaeologists have found no trace of a church. ▸

About 0.25mile (400m) after passing the short spur above the tidal island of Gateholm, the path winds through an Iron Age coastal fort. Its multiple defensive banks, enhanced by a tangle of bramble, are easily recognisable and enclose a relatively large area.

The red sandstone first seen on Gateholm runs below the cliffs, a chaos of fractured slabs and broken boulders hammered by the full force of the Atlantic waves. The island off the point ahead is Skomer and to the left is Skokholm, whilst further out to sea, about 7 miles (11km) away, is Grassholm Island. Both Skomer and

If you do venture across to Gateholm, make sure you know which way the water is running, for you will have a long wait if you get cut off.

49

Along the cliffs to the Deer Park

Skokholm have been occupied in the past, the former still bearing traces of an Iron Age settlement and field enclosures, whilst the Normans managed Skokholm as a conyger or rabbit warren. They were farmed again from the 18th century but along with Grassholm are now protected as bird reserves, Skokholm being the first of its kind in the world. It was founded by author and naturalist Ronald Lockley, who undertook the first survey for the proposed coastal footpath in 1951. Skomer is noted as hosting the earth's largest population of Manx shearwaters, whilst Grassholm is the second largest gannetry in the world, where the birds nest in such numbers that the swarming gannets have the appearance of a volcanic plume of smoke when seen from the mainland.

Before long the cliffs turn above Deadman's Bay and the path passes through a gate onto the western tip of the

Marloes peninsula, crossing the head of a glacial melt-water rift that separates it from the main run of the land. This natural gulf was exploited by Iron Age folk, who added to its defensive capability by building a stone wall to secure the headland. In the 19th century Lord Kensington enclosed the promontory with a second wall, when it became known as the 'deer park', although there is no evidence that such animals were ever kept here. Several paths meander across, but the best views are to be had from the one perambulating around the point above the much-fractured cliffs, climbing at the far side to the former coastguard lookout station. Dropping from there, the way crosses the rubble of the prehistoric defences and emerges through the park wall onto a lane above Martin's Haven.

Lockley Lodge, just up the hill, was the temporary refuge of Ronald Lockley when the sea proved too rough for him to cross to his island home on Skokholm, and is now a gift shop and information centre for the Dyfed Wildlife Trust.

Boats leave Martin's Haven for the offshore islands

Another information centre lies beside the path down to the cove, where there is a small exhibition about the Skomer Marine Nature Reserve. The sea surrounding Skomer is rich in underwater life – star fish, sea slugs, squirts, sponges and coral – a marine abundance that some might more usually associate only with tropical seas. But currents from the south temper the water here and many warm- and cold-water species meet at the respective limits of their range. Although it is necessary to delve beneath the waves to appreciate much of this, one creature you will have no difficulty in spotting is the Atlantic grey seal. Nearly 25 per cent of the world's population arrive each year to pup around the Pembrokeshire coast, many of them choosing coves around the Marloes peninsula. Take a boat trip from St Martin's Haven and you'll see even more as they bask off the islands or haul themselves onto rocks and shingle in the multitude of tiny coves.

The onward route is down to the left; immediately beyond the toilets look for a stone set into the wall. Faintly inscribed with a ringed cross, it was discovered during the construction of the wall and is probable evidence that early Christians used the cove as a landing place. Approaching the tiny beach, the Coast Path leaves on the right, a short climb taking you back onto the cliff.

There is a great view across the vast sweep of St Brides Bay as you follow the coast to Musselwick Sands. Eventually the path turns into a shallow gully above the bay and falls to a junction. To the left, you can get down to the beach, a splendid expanse of golden sand that is often deserted. The way back, however, lies to the right, signed 'Marloes'. At the top of the gully, turn right onto a field track and follow that up to a lane. Go right again and after walking for 0.5mile (800m), just before reaching a cottage, turn off onto a gravel track, which leads back to the car park.

WALK 8
St Brides and Musselwick

Start	St Brides Haven (SM801108)
Distance	4.5 miles (7.2km)
Time	2.25hr
Height gain	620ft (190m)
OS map	Explorer OL 36 South Pembrokeshire
Parking	Car park
Route features	Coastal path and field paths
Public transport	Seasonal bus service to St Brides
Refreshments	Lobster Pot Inn in Marloes and seasonal ice-cream van at St Brides
Toilets	By car park at St Brides

There is a fine stretch of coast between St Brides Haven and Musselwick Sands around the point of Nab Head. It borders the St Brides Castle estate, through which the outward leg of the walk runs.

The splendid beach at Musselwick is rarely busy and is an excellent place to linger for a picnic, or alternatively you might stop at the village pub in Marloes.

Walk through the churchyard past the western end of the church, leaving by another gate to continue at the field periphery beyond. Cross a drive leading to St Brides Castle and keep ahead beside a wall past a clump of scraggy trees to a kissing gate on the left. Cross a farm track to another gate opposite and carry on at the perimeter of successive fields until you emerge over a final stile at a junction of tracks.

Go right, but then after 200yd turn off left through a gate onto a grass track climbing alongside the hedge. Bear left at the top corner to cross a stile and carry on up the hill from field to field with the hedge now on your right. Coming out onto the corner of a gravel track next to the Old School House, follow it ahead into Marloes.

For food and drink, you will find the Lobster Pot Inn a little way along the main street to the left; otherwise, go right to leave the village. Towards the top of the hill, look

St Brides Haven

for a stile on the right, from which a grass track accompanies the hedge down towards the coast. Go left at the bottom of the field into a shallow gully, leading to the beach below Black Cliff. If you want to avoid the reascent from the sands, bear right part-way down to continue along the clifftop.

Musselwick Sands is a glorious beach and, because of its slightly steeper approach, is less frequented than Marloes on the other side of the peninsula. Nevertheless, it is just as fascinating, and is backed by cliffs of upended, finely striated slate, washed black by the sea at their lower extremity. In the tidal zone, the razor-sharp edges have been worn smooth by the waves, which have scoured a great scoop from the base of the cliffs, and the rounded slabs and boulders are encrusted with tiny barnacles and mussels. Do

ST BRIGID

St Brides takes its name from an Irish saint, known variously as St Brigid or St Kildare, who lived around the middle of the 5th century. She entered the Celtic church as a nun and later was appointed abbess over a nunnery and monastery, which she ruled with the help of a bishop. Although said never to have left her native land, she has many dedications in Wales, her cult being promulgated by Irish missionaries for whom this cove was a convenient landing. The simple church has been restored recently and has an interesting rood staircase that emerges from the wall above the pulpit. It is not the first church to have stood here, its predecessor having fallen into the sea. The erosion is ongoing, and if you look in low cliffs at the head of the bay you will see vestiges of stone coffins exposed as the old graveyard continues to crumble.

The nearby pump house provided water for the 18th-century St Brides Castle, collecting water from the adjacent spring in a huge, covered cistern. The water was pumped up to the big house by an early paraffin engine, displayed in the small exhibition to be found inside.

be careful though, if you wander along the shore, for an incoming tide can cut you off from the path onto the cliffs.

Climb back off the beach, going left at the first junction onto the Coast Path. A steep ascent is necessary to gain the cliffs, but once over a stile at the top the onward path eases into gentle undulations. Notice as you walk that the underlying rock abruptly changes from grey slate to red sandstone, which then remains with you all the way back to St Brides. Look out too for the holes of extensive badger setts in the hedgebank and below the path.

St Brides Castle can be glimpsed across the fields, the culmination of a series of rebuildings on the site. The first house, known as St Brides Abbey, was put up in the 13th century by John de St Brides, the estate later passing to the Luagherens, an influential family in 16th- and 17th-century politics. The present mansion has its origins in a

Tower Point

rebuilding of 1739, and remained a private house until the Kensingtons left in the 1920s. It has since housed a tuberculosis sanatorium and convalescent and old people's homes, but since the opening of the Withybush Hospital in Haverfordwest has been managed as upmarket holiday apartments.

Further on, the path passes alongside the double-banked defences of a promontory fort on Tower Point, then shortly turns east towards St Brides. The plain-looking 'castle' comes into view across the fields, as does the tiny hamlet and church at the head of the bay. Eventually the path turns off the cliff edge over a stile into the adjacent field. Follow the wall left, passing a second stile, which merely leads to a viewpoint overlooking the mouth of the inlet. Keep with the wall down to a kissing gate and on past a picnic area back to the car park.

WALK 9
St David's and St Non's

Start	St David's (SM752252)
Distance	3 miles (4.8km)
Time	1.5hr
Height gain	540ft (165m)
OS map	Explorer OL35 North Pembrokeshire
Parking	Seasonal park and ride at National Park Information Centre
Route features	Field tracks and coast path
Public transport	Bus service to St David's
Refreshments	Cafés and pubs in St David's
Toilets	At car park and in St David's

Leaving the ancient city of St David's – the smallest in the land – the walk heads for the coast at St Non's, which tradition holds as the birthplace of David, and then follows the coast to Porth Clais, the place of his baptism and the ancient port of St David's.

For over 15 centuries St David's has been a place of pilgrimage, for it was here that Dewi Sant settled his small monastic community by the banks of the River Alun.

The influence of David's example continued to grow after his death and, in time, a splendid cathedral was erected over his relics, whilst the medieval bishops had their residence beside it in a palace no less magnificent. The wall enclosing the cathedral precincts was erected in the 13th century by Bishop Bek, but of the four gateways only the Porth-y-twr (overlooking the cathedral) remains. It was also Bek who began the palace that stands across the river; a residence befitting his bishop's status in which he could suitably entertain the nobility arriving amongst the pilgrims. Over the next two centuries his successors lavishly extended the palace, and it was said that its banqueting hall could accommodate all the bishops in Europe.

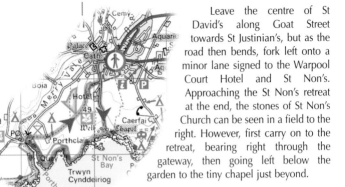

Leave the centre of St David's along Goat Street towards St Justinian's, but as the road then bends, fork left onto a minor lane signed to the Warpool Court Hotel and St Non's. Approaching the St Non's retreat at the end, the stones of St Non's Church can be seen in a field to the right. However, first carry on to the retreat, bearing right through the gateway, then going left below the garden to the tiny chapel just beyond.

Already sacred when St David was born here to St Non around AD520, the place began to attract Christian pilgrims as his cult became established. His birth was marked by a thunderstorm

ST DAVID'S CATHEDRAL

After David's death (around AD589) the shrine containing his relics became a place of pilgrimage. Tyddewi, the 'house of David', grew rapidly in importance, but its wealth made it a regular target for the Viking raiders who became a scourge of the coast during the 'dark ages'. David was canonised in 1120. Under the more settled times of the Normans work on the cathedral began around 1176, unusually sited in a hollow beside the Alun rather than on the hill above. Even more recognition came with a papal decree equating two pilgrimages here with one to Rome, and three equivalent to a journey to the Holy City itself; the wealth generated over the next 400 years fuelled the building's extension to its present plan.

The Reformation brought an abrupt end to the cathedral's fortunes, and by the close of the 18th century neglect had taken a severe toll. The Victorian zeal for restoration came none too soon, and it is fortunate that the sympathetic inspiration of Sir Gilbert Scott preserved the building's ancient character in the works carried out. Approached from the south, its plain, unbuttressed façade gives little hint of the magnificence inside, amongst the most eye-catching features being the imposing roof of Irish bog oak enclosing the nave and the beautiful gilded decoration above the choir.

St Non's Bay

and the eruption of a spring, and a stone within the ruined chapel is said to bear the marks of Non's fingers as she clutched it during the agony of her labour. A shrine was built over the holy well, whose waters were also held to have curative powers for diseases of the eye, and the chapel continued in use until the Reformation, when the practice of pilgrimage was outlawed in this country. The retreat was founded by the Passionist Fathers in 1934, together with the tiny, simple chapel constructed with stone taken from the ruins of a nearby priory.

Leaving the chapel, pass through a kissing gate at the bottom of the garden and, dropping to a path just below, turn right to St Non's Well. Through another gate, a trod crosses the field below the ruins of St Non's Chapel, joining the Coast Path over a stile. Turn right along the cliffs, overlooking a succession of dramatic coves to Porth Clais, and all too soon turning in above its long, narrow, natural harbour. Losing height easily to the head of the inlet, the path leads out to a lane by the quay.

The tiny chapel at St Non's

Go right and then immediately right again to ascend a steep, narrow path through the gorse and blackthorn thicket cloaking the hillside. Emerging into a field at the top, strike across to a gate opposite. Continue beside the next field to Porthclais Farm. Leave left onto the end of a lane, but turn off directly through a gate on the right and follow the boundary away. Carry on in the next field to join a narrow hedged track through a gate at its far side, which eventually climbs to the Warpool Court Hotel. At a junction by the entrance turn left and retrace your outward steps to St David's.

WALK 10
Ramsey Sound

Start	Porth Clais (SM739242)
Distance	7 miles (11.3km)
Time	3.25hr
Height gain	1040ft (315m)
OS map	Explorer OL35 North Pembrokeshire
Parking	National Trust car park behind harbour at Porth Clais
Route features	Coastal path, return along quiet lanes
Public transport	Seasonal bus service to Porth Clais
Refreshments	None
Toilets	Beside car park at Porth Clais

The walk begins from one of the most picturesque settings imaginable for a harbour and follows a constantly twisting cliff path above a spectacular jumble of rocks and boulders, where each turn reveals something new to wonder at. Rounding the point, the way overlooks Ramsey Sound, through which the tide can race at over 10 knots, then returns along quiet country lanes below the site of a prehistoric settlement.

If we have a favourite coastal walk, this is perhaps it, for no other corner of Pembrokeshire seems to offer so much variety of outstanding scenery within its compass.

It was to Porth Clais that the Irish bishop Ailbe (or Elvis) came to baptise David, using water from a spring that spontaneously burst forth from the hillside. As David's influence spread, the well became a hallowed spot, one of the objects of pilgrimage for the many who journeyed to this hub of Celtic Christianity. Protected from storms and largely screened from the unwelcome attentions of opportunistic raiders and pirates, the harbour was a gateway for travellers and trade from Ireland and mainland Europe that remained important throughout the centuries. More recently, cargoes of limestone were brought in to be burnt in the

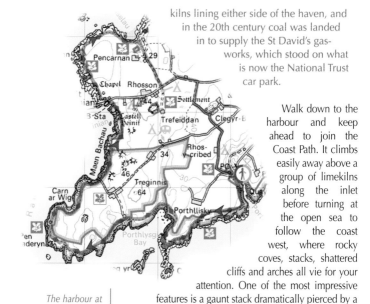

kilns lining either side of the haven, and in the 20th century coal was landed in to supply the St David's gasworks, which stood on what is now the National Trust car park.

Walk down to the harbour and keep ahead to join the Coast Path. It climbs easily away above a group of limekilns along the inlet before turning at the open sea to follow the coast west, where rocky coves, stacks, shattered cliffs and arches all vie for your attention. One of the most impressive features is a gaunt stack dramatically pierced by a slanting rectangular 'doorway'. It is not far along the coast,

The harbour at Porth Clais

but you have to look back at it to see the arch. Just offshore ahead a jumble of islets and bare rocks break the waves, whilst behind them more small islands run from the tip of Ramsey.

The absence of a road ensures that secluded Porthlysgi has rarely more than a handful of people pottering around the rocks and pools below its cliffs, or simply enjoying the sweep of sand filling the superbly sheltered beach. Yet during the latter part of the 6th century this was the scene of an invasion when an Irish warlord, Lysgi, arrived to establish himself on the peninsula. Not surprisingly his intrusion was unwelcome, but he routed the nearby settlement of Clegyr-Boia (passed towards the end of the walk). His victory over Boia is immortalised in the name of the bay in which he landed.

The coast below Porthllisky

Rounding the point behind Carreg Frân, the cliffs turn in towards Porthlysgi Bay, the path gently losing height towards the head of the beach, passing the ruin of a small building that once housed the St David's lifeboat as it reaches the shore. The climb away is not as kind as the descent, but the clifftop is soon gained and the going is again agreeable. As you work your way onto the Treginnis peninsula, look to the small islands of Carreg yr Esgob in the centre of the bay. The middle one is pierced by a sloping, needle-like gash, which almost severs it in two. Beyond Porth Henllys, above the head of a small cove, is the scant ruin of a mill. It was fed by water from a pond created by damming the stream higher up the shallow valley.

Along the coast to
St David's Head

Climbing across the headland, the way continues beside Ramsey Sound, a narrow but treacherous stretch of water that separates Ramsey from the mainland. The fast-flowing tides that surge through are dramatically highlighted as the sea flows across The Bitches, a group of low rocks towards the far side of the Sound. Indeed, when the tide is in full spate the water levels actually appear to differ on either side of them. None of this seems to inconvenience the seals, however, who invariably drift and bob offshore around the point. Another common sight is a resident school of porpoise that patrols the channel, the graceful creatures often leaping and diving amongst the waves.

Around the point at Penmaen melyn meagre foundations and a fenced-off pit at the edge of the cliffs are curious features on this otherwise deserted corner. They are all that remain of the Treginnis copper mine, which opened around 1820. The shaft led to an adit that ran beneath the headland, and there are stories of tunnels dug under Ramsey Sound in search of valuable seams of ore.

64

ST JUSTINIAN

A contemporary of St David, St Justinian lived a hermit's life on Ramsey, preaching opposition to the increasing extravagances of monastic life. He was subsequently murdered for his pains, his body being cast into the Sound and washed ashore at St Justinian's. The roofless chapel in the field beside the road is a 16th-century replacement for an earlier shrine to mark the place of the saint's first burial, but as his cult spread Justinian's relics were taken to the cathedral at St David's.

However, the enterprise failed to realise a worthwhile return and the pit was eventually abandoned after some 16 years' endeavour. Yet the lure of copper persisted and in the 1870s another venture was begun a short way south at Porthtaflod, where the main concentrations of ore had been discovered. Although that mine was apparently more profitable, it too was soon closed following a fatal accident in 1883.

St Justinian's then comes into view along the coast, the present home of the St David's lifeboat, which is dramatically launched from the station perched high on stilts above the water. Cross the path leading to the quay below, being careful not to trip over the winch cable at the top of the incline. Shortly the vast expanse of Whitesands comes into view and the path dips to a stream at the head of a small beach behind Porthselau. ▸

Cross the stream and climb away beside it to meet a track at the top. Turn right, and walk out past a small caravan site to reach a lane. Go left, and at the next junction, right, keeping with the lane as it winds below a prehistoric hillfort, Clegyr-Boia. Walk ahead at a crossroads and follow the narrowing lane down to Porth Clais.

Much of today's 'busyness' at the tiny landing at St Justinian's is due to it being the departure point for trips to Ramsey. You must book in advance at St David's and can either spend a day on the island – an RSPB sanctuary – or join one of the exciting voyages that explore the cliffs and sea caves around its coast.

WALK 11
St David's Head and Carn Llidi

Start	Whitesands Bay (SM733271)
Distance	4.25 miles (6.8km)
Time	2.25hr
Height gain	990ft (300m)
OS map	Explorer OL35 North Pembrokeshire
Parking	Car parks at Whitesands Bay and at St David's National Park Information Centre (seasonal park and ride)
Route features	Coastal and hill paths
Public transport	Seasonal bus service
Refreshments	Drinks available at Whitesands Bay
Toilets	By car park at Whitesands Bay

On a coastline where superlative descriptions justifiably are the norm, the bleak ruggedness of St David's Head has a beauty all its own.

An eruption of fractured primordial rocks pointing resolutely to the open sea, St David's Head is a place where the elements of creation come vividly together. Earth and fire have forged the ground beneath your feet, from which wind and water has wrought a landscape of awesome loveliness. The changing seasons bring their individual charm, with the fresh greens and delicate pastels of spring, brilliant yellows and heady scents in summer, and a richly burnished cloak for autumn. Even winter is not without attraction, for in the shelter of countless cracks and crevices you will find small flowers defying the natural order.

Leave the car park through a gate by a pair of telephone boxes, rising beside a rough field past a low mound in the middle, the site of a Celtic chapel dedicated to St Patrick. The way continues to climb above Porth Lleuog, the bays separated by upended slabs of rock striding into the sea and which look like some petrified prehistoric creature. Beyond, the route passes onto the open heath of St David's Head.

ST PATRICK

Legend tells that in the course of his wanderings St Patrick found this place and, deeming it so pleasant, determined to settle here. However, an angel came to Patrick saying that there was greater work for him to do, and showed the saint another land across the sea to which he should go. Patrick, trusting to God's purpose, set sail from the beach and took Christianity to the people of Ireland. A small oratory used to stand on the spot where he received his vision, but it has long since disappeared and a small plaque is now all that identifies it.

After topping the crest, descend into a wide, shallow valley, and as you lose height look to the skyline ahead for a glimpse of Coetan Arthur, a dolmen that will be seen at close quarters later in the walk. Cross the stream above the beach at Porthmelgan, then climb again to the left, the path rising along the slope of the promontory. As you approach the tip of the headland the path passes through the ditch and stone bank ramparts of an Iron Age settlement. Just beyond are several collapsed circular stone walls, the remains of dwellings that would have been roofed with wood and thatch.

Evidence of man's presence since the earliest times lies all around. Cromlechs here and below the summit of Carn Llidi date from the Neolithic period some 5000 years ago, whilst the defended settlement on the tip of the headland was the focus of an Iron Age farming community that tended the slopes of the valley behind the beach at Porthmelgan. The outlines of old field systems can still be discerned amongst the bracken and heather before the summer growth takes effect. During the Bronze Age, around 1500BC, copper and gold was landed from Ireland, to be taken overland on a trackway that ran along the Preseli Hills.

Coetan Arthur

Retrace your steps past the hut circles and through the defences, but now keep ahead on the high ground of the ridge. Several indistinct paths wander along the top, and (dependant upon the one you take) the burial chamber Coetan Arthur will very soon appear on either the left or right.

Keep ahead, presently passing a stone cairn marking the high point of the ridge. A curious drain dropping over the cliffs below served a coastguard lookout that once occupied the spot. Beyond, the way gently falls to a shallow dip. Bear right, cutting a corner of paths and then turning from the coast to rise over the eastern shoulder of Carn Llidi.

Approaching the crest, an unmapped path leaves to the right, winding through the heather and gorse below the northern face of the hill. Several narrower paths then branch off to the summit, which at its eastern end involves a scramble. However, just beyond the highpoint there is an easy path up a grassy gully to the summit ridge.

Alternatively, an easier way up (although longer) is to carry on along the main path over the crest. It drops beyond to a gate, but instead of going through, turn right on a path skirting the southern slopes of Carn Llidi. Eventually, at a junction above the Youth Hostel, go right, and then at a second junction a little further on, bear right again. The track winds up onto the western end of the hill by two dolmens.

Despite its diminutive height of barely 520ft (160m), Carn Llidi has a summit that many a full-grown mountain would envy, craggy, buttressed and commanding a view for miles around. Like its lesser companions that break the otherwise level plain, it is a monadnock, the adamantine core of a long-extinct volcano standing proud of the land as it once did from the ancient sea in which it was born. From the top, the panorama is utterly splendid in every direction, stretching in the west to the distant Wicklow Mountains of Ireland.

The view from the summit of Carn Llidi

Offshore, beyond Ramsey, lies a string of tiny islands, some hardly more than a lone rock barely breaking the waves at low tide. They are collectively known as the Bishops and Clerks and have presented a danger to passing shipping for as long as man has sailed these waters; even Ptolemy knew of their existence and described them as the Octopitarum, the 'eight perils'. However, it was not until 1839 that a light was installed on Em-sger, the South Bishop Rock, then manned by keepers but today operated automatically from the area's main station on St Ann's Head to the south. Carn Llidi's remote position and unrivalled prospect occasioned its conscription during two world wars, harnessing infant technology for the defence of the country. In World War I a hydrophone listening station was established to detect the passing of submarines off the coast, whilst in the next conflict a radar post was set up to give early warning of enemy planes and shipping.

Follow (or return along) the rocky top to its western end, where concrete foundations are all that remain of a wartime lookout station. Drop off the ridge right and pass beneath them to find some more concrete footings, where tucked in the rocks below you will find two small dolmens. Leave along a broad descending track, which shortly curves around to a junction.

Go sharp right to crest a rise. At a fork just beyond the corner of a wall, bear left, the path still dropping and soon merging with another from the right. At an obvious junction lower down turn left and, at the next crossing, go left again. You are now retracing your outward route. Simply follow the path back to Whitesands.

WALK 12
Around Ynys Barry

Start	Aber Eiddy (SM796312)
Distance	3.75 miles (6km)
Time	2hr
Height gain	685ft (210m)
OS map	Explorer OL35 North Pembrokeshire
Parking	Car park behind beach at Aber Eiddy
Route features	Coastal footpath
Public transport	Seasonal bus service to Aber Eiddy and Porthgain
Refreshments	Café and inn at Porthgain, seasonal ice-cream van at Aber Eiddy
Toilets	Aber Eiddy and Porthgain

The route follows the coast from Aber Eiddy to Porthgain, where a choice of café or pub makes it a convenient stopping place. Although the inland return is a pleasant stroll, the objective of this walk is the coast, which as well as having great character and natural beauty is dotted with the relics of massive 19th-century quarrying operations.

Leave the car park through a gate at its northern end, passing the end of a ruined terrace of cottages to reach a path that rises left onto the headland. It then shortly divides, the left branch leading to the quarries and Blue Lagoon.

Although a shorter ramble, this walk can readily be combined with Walk 13 (between Porthgain and Aber Draw) to make a full day's excursion.

An all-but-deserted hamlet overlooking a beach of dark grey sand, Aber Eiddy is an enigmatic place. A row of crumbling, roofless cottages presents a shoulder to the sea, as if oblivious of the spectacular sunsets that can be seen from the shore. Perhaps they were built that way with a more practical thought in mind, to expose less of a face against the ferocious gales that can be funnelled by the bay. In the 19th century it was a thriving place, the cliffs at the northern end being quarried for slate, some of which was exported from the shore in boats that were beached at low tide. This time-consuming process was superseded when a tramway was built along the valley behind, curving beneath the high ground of Ynys Barry to the neighbouring inlet of Porthgain, where there was a proper harbour. By the beginning of the 20th century production was no longer economic and the quarries finally closed in 1904, most of the cottages being abandoned shortly after because of lack of work. One tale relates that the decline was hastened by an outbreak of typhoid, unwittingly brought into the village by the travelling grocer. The quarry, however, was given a new lease of life when an opening was blasted through the rock to the sea, and it was used by fishermen as a safe harbour, the Blue Lagoon.

Abereiddi Bay

Return to the fork and take the other path, which climbs onto the cliffs. After the initial ascent, the onward path allows easy walking and winds above successive deeply indented bays, each separated from its neighbour by rugged, finger-like peninsulas that project far into the sea. The first bay, Traeth Llyfn, is the largest and has a splendid sandy beach, which, because it requires a short walk, is often quite empty. Access at one time was by a flight of stone steps cut into the cliffs by Italian prisoners of war, but erosion and weathering have made them unsafe and their replacement is the starkly functional metal staircase that now graces the cliffs.

Beyond Porth Dwfn the path passes above massive quarries and caves from which stone, slate and clay were excavated and taken to Porthgain, whilst further on you can see the ruins of tramways and quarry buildings. Although several minor paths wind through the workings, the onward route ahead is clear and eventually winds around to the top of the cliffs overlooking Porthgain. A flight of steps leads down to the harbour. ▶

You can return over Ynys Barry to Aber Eiddy. Amble along the lane away from the harbour, leaving the village towards Llanrhian. After less than 0.5 mile (800m), bear right off it and then keep right on a track that leads to the Ynys Barry Country Hotel. Carry on past the hotel and farm and between the fields, eventually reaching a stile at the end of the track. Follow the field edge down to the left, maintaining your direction beyond the corner to another stile below. Aber Eiddy now lies straight ahead, the path taking an oblique line of descent across the intervening gorse-covered hillside.

A navigation marker at the entrance to Porthgain

To continue along the coast to Aber Draw near Trefin, use the instructions given for Walk 13.

73

WALK 13
Porthgain

Start	Porthgain (SM814325)
Distance	3 miles (4.8km)
Time	1.5hr
Height gain	540ft (165m)
OS map	Explorer OL 35 North Pembrokeshire
Parking	Harbour car park at Porthgain
Route features	Coastal footpath
Public transport	Seasonal bus service to Porthgain and Trefin
Refreshments	Inns at Trefin and Porthgain, where there is also a café
Toilets	Porthgain

This walk follows the cliffs to the east of Porthgain and can either be undertaken on its own, or incorporated with that from Aber Eiddy (Walk 12) to create a longer ramble.

Porthgain is a splendid natural harbour, and before the 19th century it served as a quiet fishing port. However, the proximity of fine quality stone for building and roads, slate for roofs and clay suitable for brick manufacture – all in high demand for the growing industrial cities – transformed the place into a hive of tumultuous activity. For 100 years the air was filled with dust, noise and smoke, but economic depression and remoteness from the railway system changed its fortunes, and once more it became an almost silent backwater. Yet it remains a fascinating place and a superb spot from which to explore the natural beauties of the coast.

Porthgain was noted for the fine granite that outcrops in the cliffs to the east. It was exported to London, Liverpool and other great cities for use in the construction of grand Victorian buildings; splendid office blocks, imposing town halls and extravagant

Boats stranded in the harbour at low tide

museums and libraries. With the advent of the motor car, improved roads became necessary, and the granite was then crushed into chips to make the new tarmacadam surfacing, the stone stored in great hoppers so that it could be loaded directly into the holds of the waiting ships. A brickworks was established, taking advantage of a seam of fine clay that also ran through the cliffs. The harbour developed during the middle of the 19th century, and more than 100 ships were engaged in shipping out stone and bricks. Decline came with the economic depression that followed the Great War. Porthgain's position was not helped by the fact that coastal trading diminished in favour of the much quicker railways, which could more conveniently serve the inland markets.

Join the Coast Path as it climbs away above the eastern side of the harbour, heading towards a white-painted navigation marker, one of a pair built to guide boats into the narrow inlet. Turning the point and then shortly passing the ruined buildings of a small,

A tiny stream once powered a mill at Aber Draw

abandoned slate quarry, the path undulates onward along the coast. The clifftop scenery is nothing but impressive, particularly the stretch sweeping behind Gribinau and past the massive detached stack of Ynysfach. At Pwll Crochan the path dips above the shallow bay, then continues across the fields towards a farm, Swyn-y-Don, passing a stone circle in the field as you approach. Despite its romantic appearance, it is of modern construction and not a relic from prehistoric times. Skirt the buildings on their left to emerge over a stile onto a lane.

The return lies up to the right, but if you have time walk down to the tiny creek of Aber Draw. Overlooked by the ruin of a small mill, typical of the many along the Pembrokeshire coast that harnessed the small streams falling to the sea, it is an idyllic spot to while away an hour or two. ▸

Hardy walkers will want to make the return under their own steam, so follow the lane back up past Swyn-y-Don. After 0.33 mile (500m) look for a waymarked stile on the right and strike a left diagonal across the field to a gate at the far side. Keep ahead by the boundary, later joining a track that eventually winds to Henllys Farm. Stay with the track, which then crosses a stream before curving below holiday cottages at Felindre House.

To return to Porthgain, go right over a stile beside a gate on the bend and walk down to a kissing gate into the corner of a field. Follow its right-hand edge to the bottom, passing through more gates to reach a stream. Cross by a plank bridge and walk left, where a track leads back into the village.

To return to Aber Eiddy (see Walk 12), carry on around the bend to a second stile a few steps further on. Strike across the field to a stile in the distant corner, and then keep straight ahead in the next field, dropping out at the far side onto a lane. Refer now to the instructions concluding Walk 12 as you follow the track back over Ynys Barry, which lies just along the lane to the left.

The village of Trefin has the attraction of a pub, and lies a little further along the lane. If you decide the walk back is then a step too far, you can – in summer – catch the Strumble Shuttle from there to either Porthgain or Aber Eiddy.

WALK 14
Aber Mawr and Penmorfa

Start	Aber Mawr (SM884348)
Distance	3.25 miles (5.2km)
Time	1.75hr
Height gain	620ft (190m)
OS map	Explorer OL 35 North Pembrokeshire
Parking	Limited roadside parking above Aber Mawr
Route features	Field and woodland paths, which in places may be muddy, coastal footpath; some climbing
Public transport	Seasonal bus service passes nearby at Tregwynt
Refreshments	None along the walk, but there is a café at nearby Tregwynt Woollen Mill
Toilets	None

A profusion of paths offer several possibilities for fine walks in this area, and the two suggested from Aber Mawr (Walks 14 & 15) can be undertaken as separate excursions or completed in a single 'figure of eight'.

The coast and hinterland around Aber Mawr are rich in both scenic beauty and an abundance of relics that conjure an intriguing history. Although different in size, the neighbouring beaches of Aber Mawr and Aber Bach hold much in common; both have shingle storm beaches backed by marsh, and the sheltered valleys behind are cloaked in lush native woodland. Aber Mawr, the largest of the two bays, might have become a major port had Brunel's plans to build a harbour here come to fruition, and the overgrown remains of preparatory works can still be found hidden amongst the trees. The coast itself is no less intriguing and boasts a run of spectacular cliffs and broken rocks with a couple of out-jutting headlands that offered defensible sites for Iron Age settlers.

From the turning circle at the end of the lane, pass through the left-hand one of the two gates. Walk down to the beach and across the stark shingle deposit at its head. Carry on at the far side up a narrow, sunken path that climbs between banks towards the headland above. Turning before a narrow slate bridge (a remnant of

Brunel's endeavours to create a steamship port in the bay) the way rises to a crossing path. Go right over the bridge and on through a gate.

Aber Mawr is a fascinating place. In the 1840s the Great Western Railway Company commissioned Isambard Kingdom Brunel to build a railway from Swansea to Fishguard to connect with boats from Ireland. However, after work had begun, the site of the port was switched to Aber Mawr. Several reasons could have prompted the change; conceivably, with the threat of invasion by France, it was deemed tactical to reserve the safer harbour at Fishguard for naval use. The potato famine had also severely damaged the Irish trade, and the deeper water here might have better suited a transatlantic terminal; or perhaps the softer rock at Aber Mawr promised easier construction. Work began in 1848, and many vestiges still lie concealed in the woodland behind the valley. However, within three years the plan changed yet again, possibly because of the difficulties encountered in bringing the railway through Treffgarne Gorge, 8 miles (12.9km) to the southeast. Brunel turned south to build his harbour at Neyland instead.

Shortly the path splits; take the left branch and continue climbing to another gate, where a broader track takes the onward route to the right. Unpolluted by chemical weedkillers, fertilisers and pesticides, and receiving only the occasional cut-back to keep the track open, the high hedgebanks are a botanist's delight. Even if you know little about wildflowers, you cannot help but be astounded at the sheer variety of plants growing here. These in turn attract butterflies, bees and other

Rocks breaking the shingle bank at Aber Mawr

insects; a little further along is evidence of another resident family, the gaping holes of a badger sett.

Keep ahead past a junction and then through a gate, where the main track later turns off into a field. Now confined and almost tunnel-like in places as hawthorn, blackthorn and gorse reach over from either side, the way dips to cross a muddy stream before eventually ending at a narrow lane beside the entrance to Carnachen-lwyd Farm. Turn right.

After some 200yd look for a waymarked stile between a pair of gates on your right, and stay with the field edge down towards the coast where the tiny inlet of Pwllstrodur soon comes into view. Bound by forbidding cliffs and with jagged offshore rocks constantly washed by waves, it gives a foretaste of the spectacular scenery that lies ahead. Joining the Coast Path, follow it to the head of the cove, where there is access to a sheltered, sandy beach, exposed at low water.

When you can drag yourself away, cross the stream and climb a winding path onto the cliffs to continue above a rugged and inaccessible shore. High, sheer cliffs fall to the surging sea below, which boils amongst the debris and broken stumps wrought by the incessant pounding of the waves. That same battered appearance is reflected on the clifftops, where stunted gorse and blackthorn pitch grotesquely back from the sea, scorched by the salt-laden wind that drives the winter storms. The flowers on the other hand appear undaunted by these harsh conditions and in spring and summer everywhere is daubed with splashes of blue, pink, yellow and white.

There is a final view back west along the coast as you turn the point above Trwyn Llwynog, whilst just ahead lies another splendid headland, Penmorfa. The promontory was the refuge of an Iron Age tribe, and offered a relatively large area that could be easily defended across the narrow neck. The bank and ditch earthwork, even without the accentuation of the 'modern' stone and earth field boundary, remains prominent today. However, the sloping cliffs on the eastern side could have been a mixed blessing, for whilst giving easy access to the sea for fishing – or perhaps an escape route – they might also have been exploited as a 'weak spot' by enemies.

Approaching Aber Mawr you meet your outward track, dropping through a gate to a junction above Brunel's bridge. You can now either carry on ahead and pick up the instructions for Walk 15, or simply turn left and return across the beach to the parking area.

Penmorfa and Castle Coch

WALK 15
Aber Mawr and Aber Bach

Start	Aber Mawr (SM884348)
Distance	2.5 miles (4km)
Time	1.25hr
Height gain	330ft (100m)
OS map	Explorer OL 35 North Pembrokeshire
Parking	Limited roadside parking above Aber Mawr
Route features	Field and woodland paths, which in places may be muddy; some climbing
Public transport	Seasonal bus service passes nearby at Tregwynt
Refreshments	None along the walk, but there is a café at nearby Tregwynt Woollen Mill
Toilets	None

This short walk linking the adjacent bays of Aber Mawr and Aber Bach by following the richly wooded valleys behind, can be undertaken either on its own or in conjunction with Walk 14.

As well as passing more evidence of Brunel's attempts to turn Aber Mawr into a port, this walk allows exploration a little further along the coast.

As with Walk 14, go through the left-hand one of the two gates leaving the turning circle at the end of the lane and drop across the head of the beach. At the far side, you can either turn left on a path following the base of the valley, or climb ahead to a junction and join the end of the first route by Brunel's stone bridge, there turning left on a parallel path.

The tiny cottage at the end of the lane above Aber Mawr has an unusual claim to fame. In 1883 a submarine cable was laid across the Irish Sea to provide telegraph communication between Ireland and Wales. The cable was brought ashore and connected to the land line within the cottage. Some years ago, when the road was being repaired, part of the original cable was discovered and found to be still in perfect condition.

Both paths lead into the splendid woodland that fills the valley, shortly combining near an old quarry where some of the stone was cut for the unrealised harbour works. Over a stile, the way breaks out across an open meadow, briefly entering trees again at the far side before ending through a gate onto a lane.

However, just before joining the lane, turn sharp left across a stream and pass through a gate into a pasture. To the left, another gate takes you back into the trees, very soon reaching a waymarked junction. Walk right, climbing steeply to a second junction higher up and go right again, passing more relics of Brunel's enterprise as you wind to the top of the wood. Emerging over a stile into a field, follow the hedge left to the corner. Instead of then joining the lane, cross to a gate entering the adjacent field and strike out to its far corner by Tregwynt Farm. Walk through to the access track and follow it right to meet a lane. Go left, dropping to a junction at the bottom of a magnificently wooded valley.

The quick but nonetheless delightful way back is through the trees along the lane to the left, but an alternative takes in the quiet, smaller bay of Aber Bach. Carry on a little further, climbing past the next junction (which, incidentally, leads to Tregwynt Woollen Mill, where there is a tearoom) to a cottage on the left, called simply Ty Newydd or 'New House'. Turn off along the adjacent track, keeping your eyes open for some unusual sculptures hiding amongst the trees. Beyond a small cottage at its end, carry on along a narrower path, the sound of crashing waves soon heralding your arrival at the coast. After another cottage, the way slopes to the beach, where stepping stones take you across the stream emanating from the valley behind. At the far end of the shingle climb to a path, which rounds the headland of Pen Deudraeth before ending at the turning circle above Aber Mawr.

Aber Bach's shingle beach

The beaches at both Aber Mawr and Aber Bach are backed by high banks comprised of large shingle which, frustrating the flow of the streams coming down the valley, create marshy areas behind. Although having the appearance of permanent geological features, they are relatively recent and were only thrown up in 1859 after a single ferocious storm hit the coast.

WALK 16
Strumble Head

Start	Strumble Head (SM894411)
Distance	12.5 miles (20.1km)
Time	6.5hr
Height gain	2320ft (705m)
OS map	Explorer OL 35 North Pembrokeshire
Parking	Car park at Strumble Head
Route features	Rugged coast path, several steep climbs; the inland section mainly along farm and field tracks
Public transport	Seasonal bus service to Strumble Head and Harbour Village
Refreshments	None
Toilets	None

Although the longest of the walks in this book, there is nothing difficult about its undertaking. The scenery is amongst the finest along the whole Coast Path, enhanced in spring and early summer by countless wildflowers. In late summer many of the inaccessible coves below the cliffs echo to the almost human wails of hungry seal pups awaiting the return of their mothers. There is plenty of other interest too; an Iron Age hillfort, an ancient church and a collection of cromlechs are just some of the features passed along the way.

There is a choice of starting points: Strumble Head (as in the text); a small car park below Garn Fawr; or Harbour Village above Goodwick. By using the Strumble Shuttle you can optionally undertake just the coastal section of the walk.

The lighthouse on Strumble Head was erected in 1908, and although connected to the mainland by a bridge was regarded as an offshore station because of its location on a true island, Ynys Meicel (St Michael's Island). It was built when the new harbour works at Goodwick were being undertaken, and served to guide inbound ships from the Atlantic and Ireland around the treacherously rocky Pen Caer peninsula. At one time manned by keepers – who lived within the

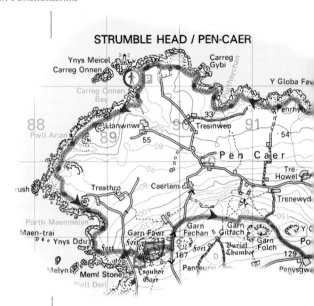

STRUMBLE HEAD / PEN-CAER

white-walled enclosure on the island – it is now operated automatically from the main station on St Ann's Head. Along the neighbouring cliffs are the remains of wartime seaward lookouts, which now serve as shelters from where you can watch for dolphins, porpoise and the occasional passing whale.

Turn left through the parking area at the end of the lane above Strumble Head to join the Coast Path south. Gently undulating, but with one or two steeper sections, the trail remains generally set back from the cliffs and eventually rises over the stubby point above Pen Brush, where relics of wartime installations lie almost hidden by ubiquitous gorse scrub. After dropping behind the well-sheltered bay of Porth Maenmelyn, it rounds another broad headland to pass above a jumble of rocky stacks.

The largest 'islet' is still attached to the mainland, and a trod leaves the main path to drop across a narrow umbilical ridge. It was defended as an Iron Age fort and the protective embankments remain conspicuous above the

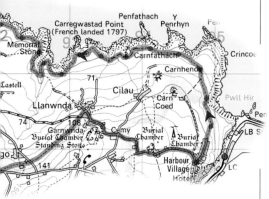

crowding vegetation. In late summer the sheltered rocky shore at the base of its cliffs overlooking Pwll Deri is invariably littered with seal pups.

Beyond, the path turns away from the coast and climbs to a lane beside the Pwll Deri Youth Hostel. Continue along the track opposite to Tal-y-Gaer Farm, bearing left where it splits towards cottages. Turn again past the one on the left as if to leave on the track, but immediately go over a stile on the right, from which a steep path attacks the bracken hillside.

Garn Fawr, rising almost 700ft (215m) straight from the sea above Pwll Deri, is a monadnock, the plug of a volcano that erupted some 500 million years ago. At the time the area was part of a vast sea in which the sedimentary sandstones, grits and shales that form the greater part of this northern coast were being deposited. The plutonic activity was not

The view from Garn Fawr

confined to a single point, and other prominent steep-sided hills breaking the landscape towards the west have the same origin. The deeply indented northern coastline of the St David's peninsula is due to the differential erosion of alternating bands of soft Ordovician rocks and sills created by less violent intrusions of molten magma.

Around the summit are the drystone defensive remnants of an Iron Age hillfort (not to be confused with the geometric modern field enclosures that overlie them), one of the most impressively located in the whole county and commanding a spectacular view in all directions. On the south and western slopes, half hidden by the encroaching bracken, are the remains of several hut circles, a small farming village that was occupied until around AD500. In our own era the vantage was conscripted as a wartime observation post, the names of its commander and builders immortalised beside the entrance. To the side is a splendid compass rose incised into the rock, no doubt fashioned to while away the long hours on watch.

Continue over the top, the path winding down the far side to emerge beside a small car park onto a lane. Head down the lane to the left, looking for a grassy bridleway off on the right, about 0.33 mile (500m) along. Follow it beside old field enclosures that are now disused and overgrown with gorse, bracken and bramble. Ignore any paths off, staying with the track as it later bends left and right. After passing a cottage, it gradually loses height to end at a lane.

Go left, but then turn off into a field on the left, just before reaching a junction. Walk away by the left-hand hedge, mounting a stile at the far corner to continue on a hedged track. Meeting a lane, cross and carry on along the track opposite, which eventually merges with a broad farm track and leads to Llanwnda Farm, where a small, country church lies over to the left.

The church is dedicated to St Gwyndafs and has several interesting features; beside the gateway is a mounting block to assist riders onto their horses, whilst from the porch there is a squint along the south aisle into the chancel. Inside, a narrow stair-case climbs from the corner of the north aisle to a high doorway overlooking the nave, once access-ing either a rood passage or a priest's room in the loft. The timbers tying the roof at the western end, merely roughly shaped tree trunks, attest to the ancient origin of the building. One of them carries a primitive carving, interpreted as the tonsured head of a monk.

From the church, walk back to the junction in front of the farm and climb away along a lane, following it left at the top of the hill and on to a junction. A bridleway directly opposite winds between the fields, passing a farm and riding stables before reaching a second farm, Pen-rhiw. Through a gate, go left and then right through the yard, leaving along a track ahead. Bear right where that later forks and walk down to Harbour Village above Goodwick, there turning left to follow the street between the houses.

The village is contemporary with Goodwick's harbour terminal below the cliffs, and whilst it provided modern homes for the people brought in to work there, its construction all but destroyed an extensive Neolithic burial site. Before the houses were built, a group of 10 chambered cairns looked out from the headland across the sea but, sadly, only two survive. You'll find the dolmens tucked behind the houses on the left, a path being signed to them from the far end of the road.

The walk now follows the Coast Path around the headland back to Strumble, and is signed ahead from the end of the street. At first remaining well back from the coast, it gently falls across a bracken and gorse heath, occasional waymarks confirming the way. Curving west above Pen Anglas, it continues along the coast, passing above a succession of rocky promontories reaching into the sea. Before long the path is drawn to the cliffs, tortuously mirroring their every indentation and undulation.

Carregwastad Point soon comes into view, but the route first swings around the back of a large bay, Aber Felin. The coves below are a good place to look for seals,

On the beach at Porthsychan

THE LAST INVASION OF BRITAIN

An inscribed stone on Carregwastad Point was erected to mark the centenary of the last invasion of Britain:

1897
CARREG GOFFA CLANIAD Y FFRANCOD
CHWEFROR 22 1797
[and below in English]
MEMORIAL STONE OF THE LANDING OF THE FRENCH
FEBRUARY 22 1797

Three shiploads of troops were dispatched with orders to land in Ireland, Tyneside and Bristol, part of a plan by the French to promote popular revolt and civil war across Britain as a precursor to invasion. Storms beset the first two vessels and the third, under the command of William Tate (an Irish American), ended up off Carregwastad. His force was ill-disciplined and badly provisioned, and on reaching land dissolved into an unruly band raiding nearby farms for food and liquor. Local militia quickly gathered to oppose them, but the hero of the day was Jemima Nicholas, a farmer's wife, who rounded up a dozen of the invaders at the point of a pitchfork and herded them into Fishguard, where there is a memorial to her in the churchyard.

but beware of the cliff edges – it's a long way down. You are shortly reminded of this as the path drops into the head of a delightfully wooded cwm. Cross the stream and climb away, joining a track over a stile. Follow it up right to a second stile and carry on above the cliffs to Carregwastad Point.

The path continues along the coast beyond, later passing Penrhyn Cottage then dipping to the head of a shingle cove, a splendid spot to linger if you have time in hand. The onward path climbs away before turning through a kissing gate to stay with the coast. Soon Strumble Head suddenly appears in front, and it is perhaps a pleasant surprise to find that you are almost there, as the path joins the lane for the final few steps.

WALK 17
Dinas Island

Start	Pwllgwaelod (SN005399)
Distance	3 miles (4.8km)
Time	1.5hr
Height gain	650ft (200m)
OS map	Explorer OL 35 North Pembrokeshire
Parking	Car park above beach at Pwllgwaelod
Route features	Coastal path, steep climb
Public transport	Seasonal bus service to Pwllgwaelod
Refreshments	Licensed restaurant serving drinks, snacks and meals at Pwllgwaelod
Toilets	By car parks at Pwllgwaelod and Cwm-yr-Eglwys

The peninsular geography of Dinas Head, with an easy finish across its neck, provides an ideal route for a short walk. Although the outward climb to the top is fairly strenuous, the views on a fine day more than amply reward the effort.

Described on the Ordnance Survey map as an island, all that holds Dinas to the rest of Pembrokeshire is a narrow strip of low-lying marshy ground, and it would take just a small rise in water level to give it independence. Geologists tell us that Cwm Dewi, the shallow valley virtually cleaving it from the mainland, was gouged out at the end of the last ice age, when vast quantities of meltwater surged through from the east in search of the open sea. Within its shelter is a strip of wet woodland, an ideal habitat for small songbirds, whilst the succession of flowers appearing from early in the year attracts many kinds of butterflies and other insects.

Begin along a track from the car park towards Island Farm. Over a cattle grid, where it then bends right, take a path on the left that climbs onto the headland. There follows a stiff and steady ascent up the sloping fields, later returning to the cliff edge as the path approaches the summit.

Inclined sharply like an up-tilted table, the 'island' is flanked on its seaward sides by progressively

rising cliffs that culminate in Pen y Fan at its north-ern point, 465ft (140m) above sea level. Almost the whole coast between Strumble and Cemaes Head is visible, with Fishguard Bay to the left and Newport Bay to the right. The cliffs here are home to fulmars and jackdaws, which wheel and soar on the air currents pushed up from below.

The view across Cwm-yr-Eglwys bay

It is now more or less downhill all the way to Cwm-yr-Eglwys, with eye-catching views along the coastal cliffs to Cemaes Head, whilst inland can be seen Mynydd Dinas and Carn Ingli, with the Preseli Hills behind. Keep your eyes open too for a glimpse of a spectacular stack standing off the cliffs below the path, aptly named 'Needle Rock'. Dropping from the hill, the path emerges over a wooden bridge onto the end of a narrow tarmac lane, which in turn leads to the tiny ruined church that gives the hamlet its name.

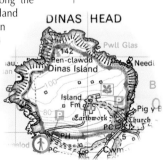

ST BRYNACH

The ruins above the beach at Cwm-yr-Eglwys are of a 12th-century chapel dedicated to the 5th-century St Brynach. Like many of the early Celtic saints, he was well travelled and made a pilgrimage to Rome from Ireland, the land of his birth. Returning via Brittany, he came to Pembrokeshire, where his ascetic serenity was disturbed when a young princess fell in love with him. Escaping her, Brynach eventually settled on the banks of the river at nearby Nevern, establishing a small monastic community. His cult flourished and there are nine churches to his name in the area, although this one has suffered from its proximity to the sea. Despite being apparently sheltered by cliffs on either side, the underlying rock is of shale and vulnerable to erosion. During the early part of the 19th century bodies were washed out from the graveyard and the chancel collapsed; then, in 1859, a tremendous storm overwhelmed the building, leaving only the west gable and its bellcote standing.

Gorse covers the hillside above Pwllgwaelod

The return footpath leads past toilets and a boat park, continuing beyond the car park through a small caravan site. Entering marshy woodland through a gate at the far side, keep ahead at a junction and walk the short distance back to Pwllgwaelod.

WALK 18
Ceibwr Bay and Pwllygranant

Start	Ceibwr Bay (SN109456)
Distance	5.5 miles (8.9km)
Time	3hr
Height gain	1040ft (315m)
OS map	Explorer OL 35 North Pembrokeshire
Parking	Limited roadside parking at Ceibwr
Route features	Coastal paths and farm tracks, which can be muddy in places; some steep climbs
Public transport	Seasonal bus service to nearby Moylgrove
Refreshments	Café nearby at the Penrallt Garden Centre, north of Moylgrove
Toilets	In the nearby village of Moylgrove

Ceibwr's narrow inlet is an abrupt break in the run of lofty cliffs that characterise Pembrokeshire's northeastern coast, and a focus for steep-sided cwms that drain the high rolling hills behind. Their size is out of all proportion to the streams that now flow through them, a product of the final stages of the last ice age, when vast quantities of meltwater were unleashed by the warming climate.

Leave the lane near the head of Ceibwr Bay along a track dropping towards Caerwen and Longhouse. At the bottom, double back sharp left almost immediately, passing the overgrown remains of a slate-built limekiln to cross a clapper bridge over Nant Ceibwr onto the beach. The Coast Path winds through the bracken heath behind and begins a steep ascent onto the headland. As you cross a couple of stiles towards the top, a pause is quite justified to admire the view back along the coast. The vista extends past Dinas Island to Strumble Head, where the lighthouse blinks its incessant message of warning. Carry on beside a cottage, cross its drive and continue at the cliff edge along the coast.

The final leg of this splendid walk drops through a deep cwm, a particularly beautiful little valley with thickly wooded flanks falling to the sparkling brook at its base. But first you must follow the coast north to another spectacular cleft at Granant, a fine airy ramble above a magnificent line of abruptly shelving cliffs.

Ceibwr Bay

Ceibwr is one of the few places along this stretch of coast where cargo could be brought ashore, small trading vessels coming and going on successive high tides. Beached at low water, coal for fuel, culm and limestone were landed, the latter two being burnt in the small kiln passed on the way down to the beach to produce lime fertiliser for use on the surrounding fields. Commodities such as grain, wood and other local produce were taken out, but by all accounts trade was not always so mundane. On dark nights when the moon was hid by cloud, brandy, lace and other luxury goods found their way ashore, avoiding the zealous scrutiny of the king's excise men.

As you round the point, there is a final prospect across the mouth of Ceibwr before the view ahead grabs your attention. The cliffs stand majestically high all along this section of coast, steep grassy slopes falling to rocky cliffs far below. In places, the cliffs rise sheer to the path, but nowhere more dramatically than at Pen yr Afr. Spectacular folding in the rocks speaks of cataclysmic primeval upheaval, from which aeons of erosion have created surreal and wonderful sculptures. Closer at hand, the grassy slopes, hedgebanks and stream channels are strewn with flowers; thrift, spring squill, kidney vetch, English stonecrop, sea campion, tormentil and stitchwort are just some that you will spot without difficulty. This is a marvellous stretch of coast, and when the view ahead is temporarily obscured by the intervening ground there is invariably one behind to savour, vindicating a moment's pause.

The path adopts a gently undulating course, but approaching Pwllygranant there is a steeper ascent, culminating in an impressive prospect. Turning into the valley, the way falls abruptly, zigzagging to a bridge across the stream at the bottom. Leaving the Coast Path the route now lies to the right, gaining height along the valley side and crossing the two tributaries of the stream higher up. The gradient eases as it enters trees, eventually emerging over a stile into a field. Cut half-left behind a cottage to a stile, and then go right along a track up to Granant-isaf.

Although the streams flowing in the valleys that broach the bastion of sea cliffs at Ceibwr and Granant are generally placid, on rare occasions they return to something of their post-glacial ferocity. The most recent inundation occurred during the night of 12–13 June 1993, when over 4.5in (11cm) of rain fell within the space of a few hours on the hills behind. The massive runoff coalesced into torrents of almost unimaginable proportions and considerable damage was done at many places along the coast. At Ceibwr the

The cliffs below Pen yr Afr

bridges spanning the stream were totally washed away, and at Granant massive landslips occurred, completely denuding the steep sides of the valley. Even the clifftops were not immune, and many sections of the Coast Path collapsed to the sea below. Yet nature's power to heal is remarkable, and by the following summer a lush green covering had softened the bare scars, putting down new roots to help stabilise the sagging hillsides.

The footpath marked on the map – cutting southeast across the fields from the farm – is, for the moment (2005), not passable, and in the meantime you must remain with the main track through the farm to reach the lane at the top. Go right, and then take the second track off on the right, dropping past Penlan to the Cadlan Valley Stud at Hendre. Keep left past the entrance drives to continue on a hedged, grassy track, which leads to another farm, Tre-Rhys.

Emerging onto a narrow lane go right, then turn left past the last barn onto a track to Cwmcornell. Where it bends by cottages, leave through a waymarked gate on the right and walk towards the old farmhouse. Over a couple of stiles to the left of the house, drop into woodland to find a plank bridge spanning a stream at the bottom. On the far bank walk downstream, shortly crossing another stile and later reaching stepping stones. Cross back to the opposite bank and continue down the valley, crossing more stiles and eventually breaking into a clearing. Ignore a track bearing right and instead keep parallel with the stream, re-entering the wood through a small gate lower down. Carry on along the wooded valley, the way ultimately leading out past a cottage. The track ahead returns you to the lane at Ceibwr Bay.

If you have time before you leave, wander along the coast in the other direction for a little over 0.75 mile (1.2km) to have a look at another dramatic inlet behind Traeth Bâch. As at Granant, the high cliffs are breached by a striking cwm, which here falls to an accessible beach. Its most striking feature, however, is a massive blowhole, a yawning chasm into which the sea pounds through a broad cave, beating against a shingle bank at the back. The valley's stream disappears underground beside it, dropping through a small cave into the cauldron to find the sea. The path to the cove passes the lip of the crater, but the best view of it is to be had from above on the opposite side of the valley, unfortunately involving a rather steep climb.

Part II
Walks in the Preseli Hills

A crow waits optimistically for scraps by the car park (Walk 19)

WALK 19
Foel Eryr

Start	Bwlch-gwynt on B4329 (SN075322)
Distance	2.5 miles (4km)
Time	1.25hr
Height gain	500ft (150m)
OS map	Explorer OL 35 North Pembrokeshire
Parking	Roadside car park
Route features	Moorland paths, moderate ascent
Public transport	None
Refreshments	Tafern Sinc at nearby Rosebush
Toilets	None

Standing at the western end of the main ridge, Foel Eryr commands a magnificent prospect to the tip of St David's peninsula and across the county to the south, as well as giving an impressive view of the quarries behind Rosebush.

Across the road from the parking area, an obvious path heads directly up the hillside. The ascent is not overly steep, but throughout most of the climb the summit looks an objective of lesser interest than a jagged outcrop of rocks on the shoulder over to the right, Cerrig Lladron. However, as you approach the apparently undistinguished grassy top, the changing perspective reveals a massive pile of stones, a Bronze Age burial.

Although obstructed by the chain of hills to the east, the view from the top is one of the best along the whole ridge and a topograph helps to identify some of the distant objects. One of the most impressive hills in the panorama is Carn Ingli to the north, part of the Preseli formation, but separated from it at the end of the last ice age by meltwater channels. The imposing burial mound on Foel Eryr is around 4000 years old and is one

Note Inexperienced walkers may find navigation difficult in poor visibility.

Foel Eryr rises invitingly beside the road crossing the Preseli Hills at the appropriately named Bwlch-gwynt, 'Windy Pass', and it is but a short and relatively undemanding walk to the top of this splendidly positioned hill.

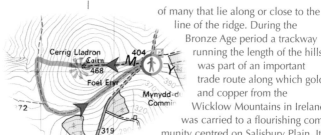

of many that lie along or close to the line of the ridge. During the Bronze Age period a trackway running the length of the hills was part of an important trade route along which gold and copper from the Wicklow Mountains in Ireland was carried to a flourishing community centred on Salisbury Plain. It is said that the barrows contain the burials of those who died during the journey.

Carry on in the same direction over the summit to pick up a fainter downhill path, which heads for the top of a shallow valley falling away towards Cwm Gwaun. At a crossing of paths marked by an isolated waymark walk left, contouring around the base of the hill. The way shortly fragments into a maze of sheep tracks, but the Right of Way leads to a signpost beside a stile in the fence ahead. Do not cross, but instead go left, following a prominent boundary earthwork to a fence. Swinging left again the path eventually returns you to the road by the car park.

The view from the top of Foel Eryr

WALK 20
Foel Cwmcerwyn

Start	Rosebush (SN074295)
Distance	5 miles (8km)
Time	2.75hr
Height gain	960ft (295m)
OS map	Explorer OL 35 North Pembrokeshire
Parking	Car park in village
Route features	Forest and moorland tracks and paths; gentle but sustained climb
Public transport	None
Refreshments	Tafern Sinc at Rosebush
Toilets	None

The highest point of the Mynydd Preseli range (and, indeed, of Pembrokeshire) lies on Foel Cwmcerwyn, barely 1760ft (535m) above sea level. Yet the summit is one that should not be ignored, for the views are quite splendid and encompass virtually the whole county.

This route begins from the former quarry village of Rosebush, winding easily up through the fringes of the Pantmaenog Forest, large areas of which are now approaching maturity and will be harvested over the next few years.

From the car park behind the Tafern Sinc, walk back to the main street and turn left past the long terrace of cottages that comprised the old village. Carry on beyond them through the now silent quarry workings and into a forest plantation.

These quarries – once one of the largest slate producers in Pembrokeshire – were started during the later part of the 19th century by Edward Cropper, MP for Penshurst near Tunbridge Wells in Kent. He became associated with the historian and

Note Inexperienced walkers may find navigation difficult in poor visibility.

The rolling bulk of the Mynydd Preseli – rising close to the sea from the north and overlooking an almost level expanse of land to the south and west – gives an impression of height far in excess of their actual elevation.

Whig MP, Lord Thomas Babington Macaulay, marrying first his sister Margaret and subsequently the widow of Macaulay's brother, another Margaret. However, he died not long after beginning the enterprise at Rosebush and his stepson John Babington Macaulay took over the quarry management, building the row of 26 cottages along 'The Street' to house the workers and their families, and even a windmill to provide power for the quarries.

Keep ahead past a junction and then shortly wind across a stream before leaving the main track onto a bridleway marked to the left. Climb away easily across open ground above a shallow valley, and on meeting a broad track at the end, continue with it to the left. Still gaining height, keep left at successive forks until you finally reach the upper edge of the forest and emerge onto the open moor at Bwlch Pennant, a shallow col breasting the Preseli Hills.

The ridge track east from Bwlch Pennant

The modern road crosses the spine of the Preseli chain a short distance to the west, but in earlier times this pass was also a thoroughfare, used as a cattle drove road, dropping out of the mountains down the valley past the hamlet of Rosebush.

Turn right alongside the gently rising fence, passing an old boundary stone as you approach the crest of the hill. Beyond the end of the forest, the broad ridge runs invitingly ahead, but the onward route now lies over a stile on the right. Climbing again, follow the fence away to another boundary stone some 50yd on. There bear left on a rising path, which snakes towards the high point of Foel Cwmcerwyn, passing the low grassy mound of an ancient burial cairn before finally reaching the top. The summit trig point stands upon a second cairn, but this has collapsed, leaving a depression in the heap of stones.

The views from Pembrokeshire's highest point are suitably rewarding in every direction. To the west is the St David's peninsula, whilst to the south lies the vast catchment of the two Cleddau rivers, with the Castlemartin peninsula beyond. Further round to the southeast is the Gower, and on the best of days the view extends to the Black Mountains, over 40 miles (64km) distant. On the summit itself are the cairns of four Bronze Age burials, one of which gave up an urn containing ashes and human bones when it was opened for the entertainment of a party of socialites in 1806.

Forest covers the lower slopes of Foel Cwmcerwyn

Maintain your heading past the summit, an obvious grass path defining a determined descent towards a corner of the forest below. Through a gate, the gradient eases and the featureless grass-scape of the upper hill is now relieved by patches of heather and bilberry. Carry on at the edge of the forest, keeping ahead lower down where the trees stand back behind a boggy clearing. Through another gate a track develops that continues beyond the forest boundary. Stay with it for a further 300yd, and then look for a stiled gap in the right-hand hedgebank. Walk away at the field edge and on over another stile before turning through a gap a little further on, from which a track winds down to a farm. Pass through the yard to the lane and go right back to the village.

Inland slate and rock deposits could only be viably exploited if the quarry was connected to the railway network, and a branch line linking Rosebush to the Great Western line at Clunderwen was opened in 1876, just a year before Cropper's death. It was extended to

Fishguard in 1899, and carried passengers as well from the station, which stood by the Tafern Sinc. The hotel was another of John Babington Macaulay's ideas, part of his scheme to establish the (by now readily accessible) village as a fashionable mountain spa. He landscaped the area with lakes, gardens and promenades, but the venture never really took off, and only the Tafern, made of corrugated zinc, remains.

Despite their size, the quarries were relatively short-lived and closed in 1906, although the railway managed to survive until the start of World War I, when its tracks were taken up and shipped to France. That too was a fated move, for the transport ship sank with its cargo before reaching its destination. Surprisingly that was not the end of the line, for after the war the track was relaid in an optimistic plan to encourage tourists. But the hoped-for regeneration failed to take place and the last passenger train ran in 1937, the line finally closing in May 1949.

The Tafern Sinc at Rosebush

WALK 21
Carn Menyn and the 'Bluestones'

Start	Parking area west of Mynachlog-ddu (SN127307)
Distance	6 miles (9.7km)
Time	3hr
Height gain	825ft (250m)
OS map	Explorer OL 35 North Pembrokeshire
Parking	Small roadside car park, west of Mynachlog-ddu
Route features	Moorland hill paths, sometimes indistinct
Public transport	None
Refreshments	None
Toilets	None

Note Inexperienced walkers may find navigation difficult in poor visibility.

Despite their proximity to low-lying villages and relative ease of accessibility, the Preseli Hills have a wonderful sense of remoteness and wilderness, qualities readily experienced on this fine walk.

Starting from the edge of the common near Mynachlog-ddu, the walk makes an easy ascent onto the ridgeway around the flanks of the unnamed hill on which lies Carn Siân. The route then wanders across the moors to the spectacular outcrops of Carn Menyn, from where stone was taken for the construction of Stonehenge. The return goes through the village of Mynachlog-ddu, where enough passing walkers might one day justify someone opening a small tearoom.

Behind the small car park, a broad, grassy path bears away to the left, rising gently around the western flank of the hill. The way later narrows, but remains clear, climbing easily to a shallow col breaking the ridge ahead. Parallel paths to the right continue the ascent, cresting the northern shoulder of the mountain and leading to a distinctive craggy outcrop, Carn Bica.

The summit of the hill lies 0.25 mile (400m) to the right, but there is no clear path to it and, although relatively high, being so flat the views are hardly worth the effort of wandering out. A few rocks burst through the grass in a feeble attempt to mark the top, but even the Ordnance Survey has failed to distinguish it with a trig point. Where the land falls away to the east, a discrete clump of rocks is reputed to be the site of an ancient chapel dedicated to St Silyn. A Lancaster bomber crashed on the hillside nearby during World War II, although nothing remains to mark the lonely site of the tragedy.

The shattered rocks of Carn Bica are much more interesting, and give a foretaste of the greater spectacle at Carn Menyn, encountered further on. In the meantime, a circular drystone windbreak crafted from the piles of debris provides good shelter on wild days for a brief stop whilst you survey the next leg of the trek.

Due east, across the head of a broad valley, lies the hauntingly impressive Carn Menyn, a direct path striking to it across the intervening dip. However, a more interesting route maintains the higher ground, curving in an arc to the north. Begin by walking down towards a small irregular oval of standing stones.

THE LEGEND OF KING ARTHUR

Many of the rocky features in the area have Arthurian associations, for one of the folk tales in the Mabinogion tells of the legendary king's pursuit of a wild boar across the Preseli Hills. His knights finally surrounded the beast on nearby Cwmcerwyn, but in the ensuing battle the boar killed four of the knights before it was finally slain. Marked as 'Beddarthur' on the map, this group of rocks is one of Arthur's many supposed last resting places, whilst another, Carn Arthur, lies only a short distance further down the hill.

Horses graze the upland moors

Where the path successively splits keep left, and bear northeast along a trod to an outlying cluster of rocks, Carn Breseb. There, veer right, pursuing an irregular line past more outcrops and cairns, now heading for Carn Menyn. Although the path is intermittently less obvious than before, in clear weather the way is never in doubt, and finally crosses the main path to reach the rocks.

This is another thought-provoking place, for the massive 'bluestones' were taken from these quarries to build Stonehenge on Salisbury Plain, that 4500-year-old enigma of early man's achievement. Some 80 stones came from here and the neighbouring outcrops, their provenance determined in 1922 by the geologist Dr H. H. Thomas, who noticed that pink-and-white crystals of feldspar in Carn Menyn's dolerite were identical to those seen in the slabs of Stonehenge. How they got to Salisbury Plain, a distance of some 135 miles (217km) as the crow flies, is a mystery, and several theories have been put forward over the years. At one time it was suggested that the stones were merely glacial erratics, moved by vast ice sheets during the last ice age. It is now almost certain that they were taken overland to the Cleddau, down which they could be floated to the sea and around the coast, and thence along the Avon and Frome. Different routes have been proposed but this one seems the most likely, the theory strengthened by the fact that the other two 'foreign' stones incorporated within the monument have been traced to the area near Cosheston on the Daugleddau just above Pembroke, suggesting that they may be replacements for a couple of stones lost en route.

An attempt to recreate the epic journey was made to celebrate the Millennium, a stone being dragged down from the mountain to the Cleddau. But as it was being loaded the raft capsized, and the stone ended up at the bottom of the water. Although it was recovered using a crane, there was insufficient support for the project and the experiment was abandoned. Instead the stone was taken by lorry to Carmarthen where it now stands in the Botanical Gardens. However, a 'bluestone' did make the journey to Stonehenge in modern times, taken by RAF Chinook helicopter in 1989. It was one of two donated to English Heritage to mark the silver jubilee of the Cystic Fibrosis Research Trust; the other stands beside the road on the common west of Mynachlog-ddu. The standing stone on the opposite side of the road commemorates Waldo, son of a headmaster at the local school who, though not brought up as a Welsh speaker, became a celebrated poet in the tongue.

A 'bluestone' beside the road below Carn Menyn

THE 'REBECCA RIOTS'

If you detour left at the first junction in the village you will come across a Baptist chapel a short way down the lane. In the graveyard, to the right at the back, is the grave of Thomas Rees. The inscription carved on the headstone reads:

Nid oes neb ond Duw yn gwybod
Beth all ddigwydd mewn diwarnod,
Wrth gyrchu bresych at fy nghinio
Daeth Angau i fy ngardd I'm taro.

This roughly translates as 'Only God knows what the day will bring, and as I went into the garden to pick a cabbage for dinner, Death came upon me. ' These poignant words belie the rough-and-tumble of his life as a younger man, for he was one of the ringleaders of the rebellion against the toll roads, which contributed to great economic hardship for the poor. A group set out one night in July 1839 to destroy the tollbooth at Efailwen, the rioters dressed as women to avoid identification and retribution. However, Rees was a big man and the only clothes that would fit him belonged to Big Becca from nearby Llangolman, and so, the story goes, the disturbances came to be known as the 'Rebecca Riots'.

When you are ready to leave, walk back to the main path and follow it to the left, bearing left again as soon as you clear the crags bordering the western edge of Carn Menyn. Losing height, curve below them to stay well above a prominent old stone boundary, Rhestr Gerrig, about 200yd lower down the hillside, and aim for the right-hand end of Foel Dyrch, the large hill rising in the middle distance. Before long the route becomes more distinct, leading you to a gate breaking the intake wall and from which a wide grassy drove continues ahead.

Developing as a track, it leads between the fields, later twisting left and then right. Keep ahead as it joins an access track from the farm, Caermeini Isaf, and walk out to a lane, there turning right into Mynachlog-ddu. Bear right at successive junctions, shortly emerging onto the common. Continue along the lane, which will ultimately lead you back to the car park.

WALK 22
Foeldrygarn

Start	Minor lane southeast of hill (SN165330)
Distance	4.25 miles (6.8km)
Time	2hr
Height gain	640ft (195m)
OS map	Explorer OL 35 North Pembrokeshire
Parking	Roadside lay-by
Route features	Hill and moorland paths, sometimes indistinct, moderate climbs
Public transport	None
Refreshments	None
Toilets	None

Man has been drawn to the Preseli Hills for millennia, and relics of his presence are strewn across them from one end to the other. One of the most evident and easily appreciated sites is the splendid hillfort on the summit of Foeldrygarn at the eastern end of the range.

The way onto the hills is along a hedge-banked bridleway opposite the lay-by. When it turns sharply right, leave through the gate ahead and strike out from the corner, guided by a vague trod that soon becomes more definite as it settles on a sensible course up the southeastern flank of your first objective, Foeldrygarn.

The most striking feature of the summit is a group of three massive stone rubble cairns – the largest of their type to have been discovered in Wales – which gives the hill its name. The cairns were built by people of the Bronze Age, who arrived in Wales around 2000BC, and mark a sacred burial site. At first placing their dead in pottery urns and interring them with gifts of food for their journey in the afterlife, they later adopted a custom of

Note Inexperienced walkers may find navigation difficult in poor visibility.

The path up to the top of Foeldrygarn is a relatively gentle climb, after which the route makes a wandering circuit of the hill, taking you past some of the spectacular outcrops of rock that are a distinctive feature of the area.

cremation, burying the ashes beneath the cairn. Obvious too, around the summit, are rampart banks. These belong to the much later Iron Age and define three adjoining hillfort enclosures. Dotted around the site – both inside the enclosures and on the hillside surrounding them – are small circular piles or rings of stones, the remains of dwelling and storage huts. It must have been a sizeable community, for over 200 separate buildings have been identified. Evidence from archaeological excavation suggests that the settlement sprang up during the last century BC and remained inhabited until well after the Romans left Britain in AD410.

Walk past the massive cairns and then bear left to leave the summit at its southwestern corner. Descending below the bluffs of natural defences, pick up a developing path that heads towards the left-hand edge of the forest breaking the middle distance. Approaching the trees, join a broad track and follow it right towards the next prominent crags of Carn Gyfrwy and Carn Menyn.

The path to Foeldrygarn

An hour or more can easily be spent in exploring the shattered outcrops and cliffs. The place is made even more awesome with the realisation that it was from here that the massive 'bluestones' of Stonehenge were taken (see Walk 21). The outcrops are of dolerite, a volcanic rock that was forced up through the overlying sedimentary shale and mudstone. Being much harder than the rock of the surrounding hills, it is more resistant to erosion and thus stands proud in the eruptions that dot the hillside. Their much-fractured nature is due to freeze–thaw action; moisture seeps into the cracks and, when the temperature drops, expands as it freezes, gradually causing the rock to split.

Retrace your steps along the main track as if to head back towards the forest, but after passing Carn Gyfrwy turn off by a small outcrop on your right, onto a narrow path making for the rocks of Carn Ddafad-las. Pass them on their right and then aim for Foeldrygarn, the way fragmenting into sheep tracks as you steer around a marshy area. Carry on above another, smaller rocky outcrop, but after crossing a couple of springs begin to swing left in a gentle arc, dropping towards an intake wall and shortly joining a more distinct path.

Approaching the wall, the path turns right parallel to it, continuing beside a low earthwork when the wall later ends. Curving around the northeastern flank of Foeldrygarn, the way eventually meets another intake extending up the hillside. Keep ahead through a waymarked gate, passing between the enclosures and then across a stream, ultimately returning to the bridleway from which you first gained the open hillside.

Foeldrygarn from Carn Gyfrwy

Part III

Walks around the Daugleddau

The river below Landshipping Quay (Walk 24)

WALK 23
Cresswell Quay and Lawrenny

Start	Cresswell Quay (SN050066)
Distance	7.75 miles (12.5km)
Time	3.5hr
Height gain	725ft (220m)
OS map	Explorer OL 36 South Pembrokeshire
Parking	Roadside parking at Cresswell Quay
Route features	Field paths, tracks and lanes
Public transport	Bus service to Cresswell Quay
Refreshments	Cresswell Arms is renowned for its beer, and the Lawrenny Arms Hotel has a reputation for good food; there is also a tearoom in Lawrenny post office
Toilets	Beside the road at Cresswell Quay and at Lawrenny Quay

Once busy with coal barges heading downriver for the sea, the tidal creeks of the Daugleddau are now all but deserted. There are good views of the river from this walk, which also explores Lawrenny Wood, a wonderful broadleaved woodland that climbs from the water's edge. Spring and summer hedgerow flowers abound too, growing in profusion along the quiet lane used for the return to Cresswell.

The rich Pembrokeshire coal seam runs just beneath the surface straight through the area, and anthracite, a high-quality coal, was mined from the late medieval period until the beginning of the last century. It was excavated from open-cast trenches or shallow pits – called bell mines because of their shape – dug beside the river, and loaded directly onto barges or boats for transportation downriver and subsequent export around the country, and even abroad. The quay outside the Cresswell Arms developed

Note High tide submerges the stepping stones at the start of the walk; however, a detour is described. A short section of shoreline path at Garron Pill, further on, also becomes impassable at high water, and as there is no alternative you must simply wait for the ebb.

as a focus for the trade, and at one time over 20 boats were employed in conveying coal from here.

At low water the River Cresswell opposite the Cresswell Arms appears little more than a babbling stream, and can readily be crossed using the stepping stones that lie just upstream from the pub. A path on the far bank then makes for the ruins of a walled garden, by-passing them on the right to carry on a little further downriver. It then swings away for a determined assault on the valley side, zigzagging higher up to gain a stile onto the end of a track. The way continues over a second stile directly opposite. ◀

Detour When the tide is in and the stepping stones completely inundated, follow the lane upstream and cross at Cresswell Bridge. Carry on beyond the bridge to a fork and bear left towards Lawrenny. Approaching the top of the hill (before reaching a barn), turn off onto a field track through a gate on the left. There is a fine prospect across the southeastern corner of Pembrokeshire before the way later dips into the top of Scotland Wood. It ends at a gate, the low-tide route joining at that point from the left. The onward path lies over the stile on the right.

Prior to the Dissolution, Cresswell was part of the estates of the Augustinian priory at Haverfordwest, but was subsequently granted to the Barlows who were responsible for building Cresswell Castle. Its scant remains stand on the banks of the river below Cresswell Bridge.

An enclosed track gently falls between the fields, introducing the first of many splendid views along the estuary of the Cresswell River. Over a stile on the left at its end, keep on by the right-hand field edge to another stile at the bottom corner. Go left at the perimeter of the next pasture, dropping to a wood at the bottom (note that the waymarked route here differs from that shown on some OS maps). The way follows the edge of the trees to the right, later dropping left to cross a muddy stream. Climb to a stile, then cross a second stream and stile, the path beyond rising out of the trees.

Walk on at the field border, crossing onto a track at the far side and turn down once more towards a gate at the edge of the wood, but leave just before reaching it over a stile on the right. Head downfield and follow the bottom boundary overlooking the pill, carrying on at the lower edge of successive fields. After skirting the over-grown and flooded remains of old workings, keep going

above the river, the church on the hill at Lawrenny now a landmark ahead. Finally, a short causeway offers a dry-shod crossing of a wooded, marshy stream out of the fields onto a lane. To the left, it leads past the confluence of the Cresswell and Carew rivers and below the site of the now-demolished Lawrenny Castle to Lawrenny Quay.

Like Cresswell, Lawrenny developed as a harbour for the export of coal, with other cargoes such as limestone, timber and even oysters, picked from beds in the tidal river, being important too. A ship-building industry also grew up, which for a time rivalled that downstream at Milford; from the late 18th to the mid 19th century over 60 vessels of various sizes were launched. The quay received a new lease of life during World War II, when Walrus and Kingfisher seaplanes from 764 Squadron were stationed on the river, but afterwards became a backwater again until the growth of recreational sailing during recent decades. The ferry that once plied the river mouth to Cosheston remained operational until the last ferryman, 'Tom the Ferry', died in the 1960s. The licensing laws may have played an important part in keeping the service going, since at one time Lawrenny was 'dry' on Sundays, whereas the pubs in neighbouring Cosheston were open.

119

Stepping stones across the Cresswell River

ST CARADOC

St Caradoc's Church lies in the village beside the entrance to Lawrenny Castle, home of the Barlows and subsequently the Lort-Phillips family. A Victorian mansion on the hill replaced the medieval castle, but that too was demolished in the early 1950s as being impractical for modern living. The church's south transept was the family chapel, and originally contained the effigy of a medieval knight before it was moved in favour of a tomb for Hugh Barlow, one-time MP for the area. The siting of the bellcote over the middle of the church is unusual and indicates how the building has been expanded over the years, whilst inside hagioscopes or squints were incorporated so that those either side of the chancel could watch the ceremonies taking place at the altar.

Caradoc was high-born during the later part of the 12th century, but after spending some years at the court of the Welsh king, Rhys ab Tewdwr, he abandoned the sable for a life as a wandering monk. After his death at Haroldston in 1124, Caradoc's body was carried along the coast to St David's for burial in the cathedral, but a sudden storm overtook the small party as they passed above what is now called Newgale Sands. Leaving the corpse protected by a silk covering, they sought shelter until the squall passed and on returning, found the shroud miraculously dry. A second miracle occurred some years later when the corpse shifted its hand as William of Malmesbury attempted to remove a finger as a relic.

Beyond the Lawrenny Arms Hotel the roadway bends past the marine stores into a boat-yard. Successive waymarks direct you through to the left and then ahead at a crossing of tracks at the far end, finally turning you right in front of the entrance to a cottage. An undulating path continues generally ahead above the Daugleddau, meandering between twisted, stunted oaks and through a carpeting mass of bilberry and wood-rush. Eventually turned by the mouth of Garron Pill – where the trees adopt their full stature in the lee of the hill – the path drops to carry on at the inlet's muddy edge, and it is at this point that you might have to wait if the tide is high. However, it is a good place for a picnic, and there are often plenty of birds about to capture the interest. Leaving the shore a little further upstream, cross a small area of marsh to reach a lane, which to the right leads into Lawrenny.

St Caradoc's Church at Lawrenny

At a junction in the village centre, follow the lane away to the left, shortly reaching a fork before a small, white-painted cottage. Bear off right along a little-used lane, whose hedgebanks, lush with wildflowers in spring and early summer, could well have been transported from biblical Eden. Walk past Newton Farm and on to Big Pencoed Farm, where the lane swings left to rejoin the main lane. Turn right and then right again at its end, crossing Cresswell Bridge as you return to Cresswell Quay.

WALK 24
Landshipping Quay

Start	Landshipping Quay (SN009108)
Distance	4.25 miles (6.8km)
Time	2hr
Height gain	400ft (120m)
OS map	Explorer OL 36 South Pembrokeshire
Parking	Lay-by overlooking the pill
Route features	Field and woodland paths
Public transport	None
Refreshments	Stanley Arms, Landshipping
Toilets	None

Note At high tide the shoreline path at the start may not be passable, in which case follow the alternative route along the lane.

Like so many settlements on inlets along the tidal river, Landshipping was exploited as a landing for shipping coal and other merchandise.

Landshipping lies on the eastern shore of the Daugleddau, just below the confluence of the two Cleddau rivers. The walk follows the shore of the main river downstream, leaving to climb through a small area of semi-natural woodland. The return lies through the fields above, passing the haunting ruins of an ancient church.

Now remote from the main thoroughfares and hardly visited, the quiet air surrounding Landshipping belies its industrial past. Many small mines operated in the area, with coal being exported from the tiny quay. The purity of the coal meant it commanded high prices; as early as the 16th century it was shipped as far away as Spain, and was in demand for specialised uses such as drying hops and glass manufacture. Proximity to the river meant that seeping water was a constant problem, and the first steam engine in Pembrokeshire was employed in draining the pits here.

The dangers of underground working were horrifically brought home when the river burst into the nearby Garden Pit on St Valentine's Day in

Memorial to the Garden Pit disaster of 1844

Detour When the tide is in the shoreline path can be impassable. So instead, continue along the narrow lane for about 0.25 mile (400m) until you reach the entrance to Woodhouse Grange. There bear off right onto a track that, through a gate, follows the edge of a pasture above the river. When you arrive at another gate, cross a stile to the shore, where the onward path remains clear above the tide.

1844. Engulfing the galleries without warning, the flood claimed the lives of 40 men and boys, almost 70 per cent of the shift working underground at the time. The tragedy took a heavy toll on the close-knit community with fathers and sons, some barely out of childhood, dying together. A memorial remembering those who lost their lives in the terrible accident stands beside the small car park.

Begin along the causeway across the mouth of Landshipping Pill and, if the tide permits, clamber down onto the shoreline at the far side. You can then walk along the shingle around the point, continuing at the high-water mark downstream beside the Daugleddau, but be careful – the stones underfoot are often slippery. Low shale cliffs contain the extremes of the river and are overhung by the grotesquely twisted and intertwined roots of native oaks, stunted even here by the wind that is funnelled up the valley. The extensive mudbanks exposed on both sides of the river provide rich feeding grounds for an assortment of waders and ducks, whilst above normal high water many types of plants find a footing in the saltmarsh and shingle. ◄

The banks of the Daugleddau

FISHING ON THE RIVER

Fishing on the Daugleddau was also an important industry into the 20th century, using small boats and a traditional compass net. The boats would be rowed into the river as the tide flowed past, and anchored broadside in midstream by a rope. The net was suspended over the side from the end of two splayed poles held together in the centre, the 'compass', and dragged beneath the boat by the current. A taut string was used to detect movement once fish were entrapped and the poles would then be brought together and raised, bringing the net back into the boat.

Beyond the point where the two routes meet, the low cliffs give way to rough grazing, after which a wood falls to the high-water mark. As you reach it, turn from the river through a gate, following a trod climbing half-right into the trees. Through another gate at the top, a clear path runs to the right along an oak-clad hillside, where mutual shelter allows the trees to assume greater proportions than seen earlier. Further on the way makes a more direct assault on the slope, winding around at the top to emerge into a field. Keep with the left-hand edge and turn the corner, leaving part-way down over a stile onto a lane at a sharp bend.

Walk ahead to a junction and go right through Coedcanlas Farm, which, we are told, claims association with the jockey-turned-author Dick Francis. As you pass the next house, Beggar's Reach, look for a waymarked stile by a gate on the right and cross the field on a left diagonal. Pass through gates at the corner and stay by the left-hand hedge into the adjacent field where you should strike out to a stile at the far side. The onward route then lies along the lane to the left, but first have a look at St Mary's Church.

125

The ruins of St Mary's lie a short way down the hill, overlooking a small inlet. The property is private, and permission to look around should be sought from the owners living in the adjacent cottage, which dates back to the 15th century and was reputedly put up for the churchwarden. Founded at the beginning of the 14th century, the church was largely rebuilt some 400 years later, and continued in use until the 1960s. However, some early features remain in several carved stones and niches in the east wall that would have held statues of the saints. In a corner of the graveyard a number of small, sparsely inscribed stones suggest that an epidemic, perhaps typhoid, hit the small community around 1760.

Climb the lane to a bend at the top of the hill, there going ahead on a metalled drive to Prettyland Farm. In the yard, turn left through a gate, from which a short track gives into a field. Follow the hedge away to the right, eventually joining an access track from Newton Green Farm, which leads out to a lane.

Diagonally opposite a sometimes muddy, gated track takes you through to a field. Keep ahead with the boundary and turn through a gate towards its far end. Now follow the right-hand hedge towards a wood, turning the corner to drop beside it. Entering through a small gate at the bottom, go right and then left to another gate, from which intermittent yellow-topped posts and occasional gates define an obvious, if meandering, path that descends gently through the trees. Emerging onto a lane at the bottom, go right and walk back to the parking area above Landshipping Pill.

WALK 25

*Little Milford Wood
and the Western Cleddau*

Start	Little Milford (SM965119)
Distance	5.25 miles (8.4km)
Time	2.25hr
Height gain	550ft (170m)
OS map	Explorer OL 36 South Pembrokeshire
Parking	Car park at Little Milford Wood
Route features	Woodland, field and riverside paths
Public transport	None
Refreshments	None
Toilets	None

This is a fine walk, with an ever-changing character throughout the year. It begins through old, rambling woodland, which was heavily mined for coal during past centuries, and abandoned shafts lie hidden in the trees. Coal from the mines was taken away on barges, loaded from small quays, whose remains still line the banks of the Western Cleddau sweeping below Little Milford Wood which, although here a considerable distance inland, is still a tidal waterway.

Woodland has cloaked the hillside above the river here since at least the 16th century, and was managed by the traditional practice of coppicing to produce small timber until the practice became uneconomical in the 1920s. Much of the native woodland was subsequently felled in the middle of the century and replaced with closely planted conifers, a cash crop satisfying the needs of the industrial timber market. Since its acquisition by the National Trust in 1975, the softwood is being felled as it reaches maturity, leaving local species such as oak and ash to regenerate in its place.

Note The shore path may occasionally be waterlogged, and at high tide a short section is temporarily flooded, but a detour is possible via the lane.

Spring and autumn are the best times to see the woodland, whilst during the winter months the mudflats bordering the river attract a multitude of birds.

Leave the back of the car park by an information panel, along a path that climbs away beside a young plantation. Carry on at the top into mature trees, going left when you reach a crossing of paths. Keep ahead where another path shortly joins from the left, and later take the higher branch at a fork. Emerging onto a broad crossing track, go right, rising to a fork where you should bear left. Just beyond the path is crossed by the dead-straight course of an old incline, down which tubs of coal were lowered to the quayside. Carry on, curving right, to arrive at a car park.

Little Milford and Nash Woods, reached a little further on, overlie extensive coal seams that have been mined since medieval times. At first the coal was dug from simple bell pits, a short, vertical shaft around which excavation continued to the point of collapse, when a new shaft would be sunk nearby. These can be identified in the many hollows and depressions dotted throughout the woods. By the 19th century steam power made deeper mining possible, and the Frystop Colliery operated until 1948. Until the railway arrived the coal, a high-grade anthracite, was taken downriver in barges on the tide, whilst incoming craft brought limestone, which was burnt to produce fertiliser for use on the surrounding fields. You will see the kiln hidden in the trees beside the road on the right as you return to the car park at the end of the walk.

128

Turn right, but approaching a bend at Maddox Moor leave over a waymarked stile beside a gate on the left. Follow the right-hand field edge to a stile about halfway along, which crosses into a small farmyard. Go left through a gate and stay left to join a short, hedged track that opens into a field below. Carry on by the right-hand hedge, keeping ahead over a stile at the bottom to reach a stream. Cross to another stile opposite and follow a path left, winding through Nash Wood.

Approaching the far side, the path widens to a track and rises to a derelict cottage. Bear left with the track in front of it, emerging at the top into a field. Carry on along the boundary of successive fields, eventually reaching North Nash Farm. Walk on through the yard, but turn left immediately past the last building to go, not through the gate, but over a stile just left of it. Walk away with the hedge on your right, continuing through a gate in the next field. At the corner of that pass through a gap on the right and turn left to then follow the hedge on its opposite side. Leave at the far end over a stile hidden in the corner and follow a tree-lined track out to a lane opposite Llangwm Cemetery.

Coal was once loaded from the now skeletal piers

Hook Reach

Continue along a wooded track opposite, which soon narrows to a path (sometimes muddy). At a junction go left, shortly emerging into a field. Keep going by the hedge, passing into the next field and on down to a stile and footbridge spanning a stream at the bottom. A track leads out to the end of a lane at Middle Hook.

Turn right, but after a few paces go left at a footpath sign, crossing a footbridge from which a path winds past the edge of scrub woodland to a gate near a ruined cottage. A track continues across open ground towards more trees, passing through a gate to be joined by another track from the marsh. The onward way now runs as a clear track over the crest of a low hill to meet a narrow lane which, after passing farm entrances, runs to the left.

After some 250yd turn off along an old wooded track on the right, emerging through a pair of gates at the bottom above the river. The onward route can be somewhat marshy at high water, and follows the tidal fringe upstream to the left, soon passing a couple of cottages and the remains of an old quay. The riverbank path hugs the base of low shale cliffs, topped by trees whose roots dribble in crazy knotted tendrils over the edge. Later, approaching the stark wooden skeleton of another derelict pier, the way cuts behind into the garden of a cottage. Walk through to its drive and follow it uphill as far as a sharp bend. ▸

The crumbling ruins of piers jutting at intervals from the banks are reminders of a time when the river was busy with trade. During the 19th century, barges and shallow-keeled boats came upriver with the tide, taking cargoes of coal, timber and grain down to Pembroke Dock, Neyland and Milford Haven for transhipment onto sea-going vessels.

At high tide the onward riverside route becomes impassable, for the water laps right to the shale banks that bound it. The way is not blocked for long, however, and you can either wait for the ebb or take the detour. When the tide is out, leave on the bend, where a path drops back to the margins of the river and carries on upstream for a further 0.33 mile (500m). You then reach the point where the tide floods the path, and even at low water the next few steps can be very muddy. The best way lies close to the cliff.

Not far beyond a lone sign warns of sinking mud, whilst a little further on is a bench and crude shelter fashioned below the cliffs. Rough steps just before the shelter take you off the shore, the path winding on above it through the wood and becoming a track as it approaches some cottages. Bear right when you reach Little Milford Lodge, then swing left to climb along the lane back to the car park, remembering to keep an eye open for the old limekiln.

Detour At times of high water an alternative return is possible along the road, which can be reached by continuing up the drive from the cottage.

WALK 26
Minwear Wood

Start	Forestry car park west of Blackpool Mill (SN058142)
Distance	4.5 miles (7.2km)
Time	2hr
Height gain	450ft (135m)
OS map	Explorer OL 36 South Pembrokeshire
Parking	Forestry car park on the right, heading west from Blackpool Mill
Route features	Woodland paths and field tracks
Public transport	None
Refreshments	Tearoom at nearby Blackpool Mill
Toilets	For visitors to Blackpool Mill

Minwear Wood runs for some 2 miles (3.2km) along the southern bank of the Eastern Cleddau, immediately below its tidal limit.

Large areas of Minwear Wood were given over to commercial plantation in the middle of the 20th century. As with neighbouring Canaston Wood, parts of the forest are now reaching maturity and timber felling has created many open spaces. In time these will be replanted using a mix of species that will include many native trees in order to promote diversity in the habitats.

Where the land lies flat and marshy beside the water, extensive reed beds have become established, whilst a little way downstream, the falling tide exposes mud-flats, two different environments – as well as the woodland – attracting their own abundant wildlife.

A broad, forest track, identified as the 'Landsker Borderlands Trail', leaves from the far end of the car park. Later narrowing, it undulates through an as yet immature beech wood, the tall, leggy trunks striving upwards in desperate competition for the light at the top of the canopy. Beyond a stream the composition of the forest changes to fir, returning later to more beech, this time

mixed with oak. Ignore a waymarked path that shortly leaves on the left, but a brief deviation to the right a little further on is rewarded by a splendid viewpoint overlooking reed beds bordering the river.

The Eastern Cleddau below Minwear Wood

Outside the softwood plantations there is a good mix of native trees, including oak, ash, beech and holly. You will also come across others such as sycamore and sweet chestnut which, although introduced to Britain by man, have become naturalised and spread throughout the country. In early spring, before a dense leaf cover shades the woodland floor, you will find a wide range of flowers, such as lesser celandine and wood anemones. Later bluebells and foxgloves paint their own colours amongst the trees, whilst more delicate plants like wood spurge create pockets here and there. Autumn is perhaps the most beautiful time as the leaves become burnished with

133

a richness of hue hardly imaginable. It is also the season of fungi, whose strange shapes, colours and properties have, throughout history, set them mysteriously apart from any other natural flora.

Carry on through a recently felled area and past another waymarked path off left, shortly dipping into a gully, through which several streams course. At a junction of paths just beyond, the one to the right again leads to an old landing beside the river, where there is a limekiln partly hidden in the trees. As before, however, the onward route lies ahead, through a tapering natural woodland of ash and oak, interspersed with holly and other trees. After curving around the head of a stream, the way briefly rejoins the main river before turning away over a stile. After passing a number of ruined buildings – the overgrown remains of a medieval nunnery – the path breaks out into a field above. Carry on alongside the hedge, leaving beside a pond at the top onto a track that leads to

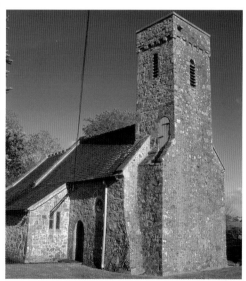

St Womar's Church at Minwear Farm

THE KNIGHTS OF ST JOHN

The Knights of St John have their roots in Jerusalem during the first crusade, one of two religious orders founded to offer protection to pilgrims visiting the Holy Land. There soon evolved within the order three separate branches directed to religious, charitable care and military ends, and the organisation amassed great wealth and power through gifts of land and property across Europe. Political jealousies and intrigue led to the disbanding of the other great crusading order, the Templars, at the beginning of the 14th century. Much of their property was transferred to the Hospitallers, whose work became focused on providing hospitality and care to the many thousands making pilgrimages to the shrines within Europe.

A Commandery or headquarters of the Knights of St John was established across the river at Slebech (see Walk 27), and the Norman knight Lodomer granted land and founded a small chapel here for the order in 1150. The dedication to St Womar is, in all likelihood, a corruption of his name. The building was extended during later centuries with the addition of a chancel, aisle and tower, and its embattled upper courses suggest that it also served a defensive role from time to time. The ruins passed in the woods as you left the river are now known as the 'Sisters' House', although early documents refer to it as the 'Systerne House'. We are told that it was possibly a hospital run under the auspices of the Commandery across the water, established to provide care for women pilgrims on their way to St David's. After the Dissolution, when the possessions of the Hospitallers were confiscated (along with those of abbeys and priories elsewhere in the country), the property was turned to secular use, and for a time became a family residence.

Minwear Farm. Through the yard bear right to a tarmac drive, walking out past a small church to reach a lane.

Cross diagonally right to a gate from which a hedged bridleway leads away between the fields. Keep ahead at a crossing field track, eventually reaching a narrow lane at its end, and there turn left, climbing to a farm. Through a gate the way continues as an unsurfaced track into a forest plantation, winding pleasantly amongst the trees. Beyond a forestry compound the way falls to meet the road, along which is the car park, a short distance to the right. However, you can avoid walking on the road by adopting a parallel path tacking the fringe of the trees on the right.

WALK 27
Blackpool Mill and Slebech Church

Start	Forestry car park west of Blackpool Mill (SN058142)
Distance	4.5 miles (7.2km)
Time	2hr
Height gain	260ft (80m)
OS map	Explorer OL 36 South Pembrokeshire
Parking	Forestry car park on the right, heading west from Blackpool Mill
Route features	Woodland paths and field tracks
Public transport	None
Refreshments	Tearoom at Blackpool Mill
Toilets	For visitors to Blackpool Mill

Despite its simplicity this is an excellent walk along the Eastern Cleddau, and reveals many picturesque views of the river.

This walk leads to an ancient chapel of the Order of St John, superbly sited on a small wooded headland overlooking the water. Another attraction is the imposing watermill at Blackpool Bridge, passed at the start, which has been restored to show some of the original equipment and houses an interesting exhibition.

As if leaving the car park for the road, turn immediately left along a path beside the entrance, marked as the 'Landsker Borderlands Trail'. Over a stile at the bottom, follow a walkway curving across marsh to a gate and continue in the field beyond to Blackpool Mill. Go past the front of the buildings and follow a track over Blackpool Bridge into the Slebech estate, turning left when you shortly arrive at a junction.

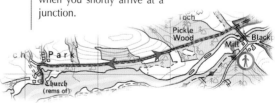

Blackpool Mill

From medieval times the fast-flowing waters of the Daugleddau and its tributaries powered many mills, and one is known to have existed at Blackpool since the 16th century. During the succeeding 200 years it worked an iron forge, the surrounding forest providing the charcoal to heat the furnaces. By the beginning of the 19th century the operation had become uneconomic and Nathaniel Phillips – then owner of Slebech – rebuilt it as a grist mill, the building that stands today. Originally powered by two separate wheels that maximised the benefits of the varying head of water as the tide changed, much of the machinery was replaced in 1901 and a water turbine was installed. The mill continued in operation until after World War II, but gradually fell into dereliction until restoration was begun in 1968.

Blackpool was the lowest place at which the Eastern Cleddau could be forded, and it was not until the 19th century that a bridge was constructed.

The track wanders down the valley above the river, sometimes through woodland and later at the edge of fields. There are intermittent views to reed beds bordering the water, which attract some less common birds including reed warblers, summer visitors from Africa, and perhaps even the odd bittern. When the tide falls mudbanks are exposed which, although visually unappealing, provide rich feeding grounds for large numbers of waders, particularly during the winter months.

After some 1.75 miles (2.8km) there is a glimpse of a large mansion ahead, Slebech Hall, before the previously straight-running track sweeps around the head of a side creek. Ignore a footpath off into the trees on the right and bear left at a junction a few steps beyond, heading back towards the river and Slebech Hall. Where the track then swings right towards the house, keep ahead on a narrower path, and when that subsequently divides fork right towards the church.

From the 12th century the Slebech estate was held by the Knights of St John of Jerusalem, founded as a religious charity to aid pilgrims journeying to the Holy City, but also undertaking the literal defence of the Christian faith. The Commandery here oversaw considerable holdings throughout Pembrokeshire, and such wealth was an obvious target when Henry VIII ordered the Dissolution of the monasteries. The Crown sold it to a powerful local family, the Barlows.

Roger Barlow had sailed with Cabot to South America, and is reputed to have been the first Englishman to land in Argentina; his brother William was prior of Haverfordwest and subsequently Bishop of St David's. The Barlows held the estate for 200 years before it passed by marriage to John Symmons, who demolished the medieval buildings in favour of an 18th-century mansion. Unfortunately his ambitions outstripped his wallet and he sold out to a Jamaican sugar plantation owner, Nathaniel Phillips, whose son (also named Nathaniel) built the mill and bridge at Blackpool. Subsequently – again through marriage – Slebech passed to a Polish noble, Baron de Rutzen (who caused upset in the neighbourhood when he wanted to introduce wolves into the forest), and then the Dashwoods, who were responsible for restoring the mill.

Being claimed as the parish church for Slebech, St John's Church survived the secularisation of the Commandery and continued in use until 1848, when the de Rutzens commissioned a new building in the hamlet of Slebech beside the main road. Ironically, that also is now disused. The tiny church – all that remains of the Knights' headquarters – is a picturesque ruin open to the heavens, and contains several interesting features. Elegant archways connect its cruciform shape and the south chapel is provided with a fireplace for the comfort of the lord of the manor. An alcove in the south wall may have held the effigies of Sir William Wogan and his wife of nearby Picton, which were removed to the new church. At the base of the tower, through which the church is entered, stands part of an ancient yew, thought to be over 1000 years old and having a girth of nearly 14ft (4.2m). Buried nearby are Sir William Hamilton and his first wife Catherine Barlow. Hamilton subsequently married Emma, who later became embroiled with Nelson. In 1955 the church was given back to the Order of St John, and an annual commemorative service is held on the Sunday nearest St John's feast day.

St John's Church at Slebech

The Hospitallers held lands on both sides of the river, the probable remains of a hostel for female pilgrims being hidden in the trees on the opposite bank (see Walk 26). A ferry would have operated between the two shores, but no such facility exists today, and without a convenient alternative route you must retrace your steps to Blackpool Mill.

Part IV
Rivers, woodland and a lake

A stile takes the path into the wood (Walk 38)

WALK 28
Carew Castle and Mill

Start	Carew (SN046036)
Distance	1.25 miles (2km)
Time	0.5hr
Height gain	80ft (25m)
OS map	Explorer OL 36 South Pembrokeshire
Parking	Car park by castle entrance
Route features	Easy all-weather track
Public transport	Bus service to Carew
Refreshments	Riverside tearooms and Carew Inn
Toilets	Opposite car park

Throwing rippling reflections across a placid pool that laps beneath its walls, Carew Castle has one of the most charming settings in Wales, an idyll exploited by the great Romantics of the 18th and 19th centuries who sought to capture it on canvas. But the castle was not built for its scenic beauty, and when Gerald de Windsor raised a tower and palisade defence for his overlord during the closing years of the 11th century, it commanded the upper tidal reaches of the Carew River. The strategic advantages of the site had been recognised long before, and the partly visible earth ditches suggest original Iron Age fortifications that probably continued to be occupied until the Normans arrived. Political winds later blew the castle into the possession of the de Windsors, who adopted the name Carew, and their descendants still hold title to the property. With the passing centuries peace fell upon the region and the stark utility of the garrison was transformed into a splendid country residence, with spacious apartments looking out through grand Elizabethan fenestrations that

Although the shortest walk in the book, this gentle stroll can still form the basis of a full day's outing, for it offers the chance to visit that most picturesque of castles at Carew, as well as a fascinating and almost unique tidal mill. A joint entry ticket is available, which should be purchased from the castle reception before commencing the walk.

replaced the dark passages and arrow slits of previous generations.

Troubled times were to return once more with the civil wars of the 17th century and the castle, held by the Royalists, was three times taken by the Roundheads, who ultimately destroyed the southern wing to prevent its reuse. Subsequently abandoned it became a stone quarry, and for 300 years suffered at the hands of local builders, stone burners and, of course, the weather. Yet enough has survived to tell its story, brought to life by colourful pageants and events that regularly take place during the summer months.

Carew Castle throws reflections across the mill pond

Begin along the metalled track beside the car park, which leads past the castle's impressive ruins. Bear right when you reach a fork after 0.5 mile (800m) and carry on to the mill.

142

The tidal mill

The fortunes of most mills lie at the mercy of the weather, optimistically looking for consistent rainfall or wind throughout the seasons. The tidal mill, however, is freed from such constraints, for its power derives from the moon's endless journey through the heavens, and twice each day its full head of water is restored. The one at Carew is almost unique (there are only four such mills now remaining intact in Britain) and was built some time before the early years of the 17th century, when the causeway first appears in the documentary record. At the head of the tidal river, it also had the advantage that seagoing boats could come right alongside and flour could be loaded directly for shipment. It underwent a major restoration at the end of the 18th century and was still in commercial use in 1937. For most of its life it has been used to grind grain for flour, but at one stage also ground bones for use as a fertiliser. It is now fully restored – although no longer grinds corn – and, with its interesting display on the history of milling, is open to the public.

143

As you then walk along the top of the dam there is a splendid view across the tidal reservoir to the castle, whilst at high tide the Carew River presents a fine prospect downstream. Low water, however, reveals only a meandering trickle contained between bare muddy banks where only light-footed birds can tread with any safety. A good path traces the way back above the far bank of the pool, from which the most romantic vistas of the castle are to be had, its reflection shimmering in the gently lapping water of a still day. Emerging through a picnic area, continue along a lane to the main road, keeping a watchful eye open for passing traffic as you then follow it across the causeway. The car park lies just ahead up the hill, but first turn off beside the Carew Inn to have a look at the so-called 'Flemish chimney'.

During the medieval period only the very rich could afford to build in stone, and even the majority of the gentry had to be satisfied with wood. Being combustible this meant that there could be no chimney, and cooking and heating was provided for by an open fire, the smoke allowed simply to seep out through the rafters or escape through a special vent – a louver – built into the roof. During the 16th century a wealthy merchant class developed who could afford to flaunt their status by the incorporation of stone into their residences. The chimney became the great status symbol of the day, with each builder striving to outclass his neighbour. A style developed in south Pembrokeshire that became known as 'Flemish', a mistaken association with the Flemish weavers who settled in Tenby during the reign of Henry VIII. The one here has survived its original house, which was demolished around 1870, and continued in use as the village bake-oven until 1927.

Another interesting monument is the Carew Cross, which overlooks the main road from opposite the pub. Standing over 13ft (4m) high and surmounted by a splendid wheel cross, the Carew monument is an impressive example of early Christian art. The intricate plaitwork of inter-twining symbols decorating its faces suggests early Celtic and Scandinavian influences, whilst a carved Latin inscription commemorates the Welsh prince Maredudd, the son of King Edwin. He was killed in battle in 1035, and with his brother Hywel had ruled Deheubarth, the Celtic kingdom of southwest Wales. The obelisk is one of the finest from the period and has been adopted by CADW (Welsh Historic Monuments) as its emblem.

Carew Cross

WALK 29
Kilgetty

Start	Tourist Information Centre at Kilgetty (SN122071)
Distance	6 miles (9.7km)
Time	2.75hr
Height gain	525ft (160m)
OS map	Explorer OL 36 South Pembrokeshire
Parking	Free car park behind Information Centre
Route features	Field paths and tracks
Public transport	Bus and rail services to Kilgetty
Refreshments	Begelly Arms and Millie's Café, as well as a fish bar in Kilgetty
Toilets	Behind Information Centre

The woodlands are a good place to look for small songbirds, often easier to hear than to spot, and whilst coming back along the old railbed it is interesting to see how Nature has muted the outlines of the old colliery workings.

After beginning through quiet forest and unspoilt woodland above the Ford's valley, this meandering ramble heads across the fields to pick up the line of the Saundersfoot Railway, relaid and converted to steam during the 19th century to serve the several coal-mines which operated northwest of Begelly.

Walk along the main street from the Information Centre into the village. Leave beyond the top of the hill and just before a road signed to Sardis to go along a track on the left, marked as the 'Miners' Walk'. At the end, go through a gate to the right of the cottage in front, and follow a trod away across a flower-rich meadow, curving left to a stile by the far corner into a conifer plantation. A short way into the trees, bear left at a skewed junction and climb beside an old bank boundary to a stile from which a narrower path runs on through mixed woodland, where lesser celandine, primroses, wood anemone, ransoms and a speckling of bluebells make a splendid springtime show. At the end of the wood, move left to a stile and carry on at the edge of open grazing, soon penetrating the hedge to join a track beside it. Continue between the fields to Penrath Farm.

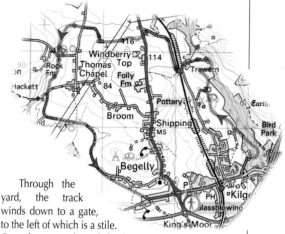

Through the yard, the track winds down to a gate, to the left of which is a stile. Over that, pass through bushes to emerge in a field and turn right to a stile in the bottom corner. Along a planked walkway, yet another stile begins a path that contours through open wood and heath above a splendid, secluded valley. Crossing a stream, the track swings right, but then some 200yd on look for a waymark indicating an obliquely rising path to a cottage, Rose Hill Farm. Follow a track away past another farm, which ends at a lane beside the railway. Go right over the bridge and carry on until you reach the main road.

Walk left; after 100yd leave over a waymarked stile on the right, crossing the field to a pair of adjacent gates. Carry on through the left-hand one, initially by the hedge but continuing beyond its end across the slope to a stile. Keep ahead at the edge of subsequent fields to Bramblehill Farm, leaving to the right along its access track.

There were two major mines in the area, Thomas Chapel and Broom Hill, both producing high-grade anthracite for export as far away as Singapore. At first the coal was hauled down to the shore at Wiseman's Bridge for loading onto

147

Primroses carpet woodland glades in spring

beached ships that were then floated off at the next tide. Output increased after 1834 when a tramway was constructed to the harbour at Saundersfoot, with further dramatic increases following its later conversion to steam. During the 1920s a decline in the industry rendered the line uneconomic, and despite a brief revival at the beginning of World War II, it was ultimately closed. The nearby main line, however, continues to run via Kilgetty and Tenby to Pembroke Dock, where it connects with the Irish ferry operating from the port.

Cross the lane at the end to a stile opposite, from which a path winds on through scrub to reach a meadow. Strike diagonally left, joining the bottom boundary into the corner, where a path develops beside a wooded stream. Keep going past a ruined mill and then shortly over a crossing track, later emerging into another open field. Carry on along the bottom edges of successive enclosures, eventually meeting a sunken lane. Turn right, then immediately left onto a broad hedge-banked track, which occupies the bed of the railway that once served the many coal-mines littering the shallow valley. Later, after passing beneath power cables, the track swings left into a field, but you should keep ahead over a stile to regain the embankment. Stay with the course of the old tramway until, eventually, the track splits. The right-hand branch enters an arboreal tunnel before ending between houses onto a road. Turn left past the Begelly Arms to the main road, carefully crossing by the roundabout to return to Kilgetty.

Both Begelly and Kilgetty were mining villages, but the latter's greater expansion was influenced by the opening of a station on the main railway line. The large open area to the south of the villages is common land, and once the traditional site of a gipsy encampment. It survived an attempt at Parliamentary Enclosure in 1855 and has become a notable wetland heath supporting such less common birds as the corn bunting and sedge warbler.

Ford's Lake

WALK 30
Canaston Wood

Start	Forestry car park west of Blackpool Mill (SN059142)
Distance	5.25 miles (8.4km)
Time	2.5hr
Height gain	600ft (185m)
OS map	Explorer OL 36 South Pembrokeshire
Parking	Forestry car park on the left, heading west from Blackpool Mill
Route features	Woodland paths and tracks, which can be very muddy in places
Public transport	None
Refreshments	Tearoom at Blackpool Mill
Toilets	For visitors to Blackpool Mill

Canaston Wood is divided by a main road, and the ramble can thus be broken into two shorter walks, one beginning near Blackpool Mill and the other starting from an alternative car park beside the A4075 (SN074140).

A maze of paths meanders through Canaston Wood, but they do not all correspond with those marked on the OS map and site information boards. However, the course followed by this walk is marked on the accompanying illustrative map and utilises commonly used tracks.

Harvesting operations are changing the character of the forest and have opened some far-reaching views through the trees to the Preseli Hills in the north. In the eastern part of the wood, the route leads past the remains of a tiny chapel and an Iron Age hillfort.

Out of the car park, follow the lane a short distance past the entrance to Blackpool Mill before bearing off right onto a bridleway rising into the forest. Beyond a broad clearing, the track gently dips and crosses a stream hidden in the trees. There a waymarked grassy path leaves on the right, climbing beside the runnel along a shallow valley. Where it levels at the top, keep ahead as a waymarked path joins from the left, but then, at a second waymark a bit further on, turn left (if you reach a gate and stile onto the main road you have gone a little too far). The path winds across the top of the wooded hill where, until the young saplings become established, there is a view north to the distant Preseli Hills. Falling at the far side, the way meets a broad forest track.

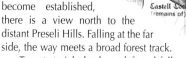

To cut straight back, go left and follow the track down to the lane by Blackpool Mill. Otherwise, swing right, soon emerging onto the main A4075 road opposite another parking area serving the eastern part of Canaston Wood. This is the parking for the second short walk.

Although planted for commercial timber production by the Forestry Commission, Canaston and Minwear are part of what was a much larger medieval forest. At the beginning of the 17th century it was described by George Owen of Henilys, an Elizabethan historian, as one of the 'best standing woods in the country'. The wood would have formed an integral part of the community, providing game and some winter grazing as well as large and small timber for a wide range of uses from boat and

Canaston Wood

building construction to fencing and firewood. By the 18th century much of the large timber had apparently gone, but the forest was still managed to provide small wood by coppicing. Such wood was ideal for charcoal production, and this fuelled a small iron foundry down by the river. In the 19th century Baron de Rutzen of nearby Slebech Hall (see Walk 27) introduced wild boar into the forest to provide sport for his hunting parties. He would have gone even further by letting wolves loose as well, but he demurred on this, bowing to pressure brought by the local community.

The modern commercial timber trees consist mainly of larch, Douglas fir and Norway spruce, many of which were planted during the 1950s and are now reaching full maturity. Harvesting is taking place and large areas are being felled, opening, for a time at least, fine views across the surrounding countryside. The subsequent replanting will increase the diversity of species and include trees that are native to the area such as oak, ash, hazel and willow, thereby improving the habitats for small animals and birds.

Be careful crossing the A4075, for traffic moves quickly along this busy road, and follow the continuation of the track into the trees opposite. After some 150yds fork right onto another broad track, which soon narrows to a winding path through a young plantation. Entering mature woodland at the far side (if it has not been felled), the way can be very muddy in places, but keep going through the trees. On reaching an indistinct fork by a three-way sign bear right, dipping across a stream before climbing to meet a wider path near the upper edge of the forest. To the left it passes through a couple of gates and then climbs to reach a junction. Keep ahead a little further, the way shared by a small stream, to find a stile some 70yd along on the left by a wire fence that forms a partial barrier across the track. In the field stands the ruin of a small, isolated chapel.

The ruined Baptist chapel

The tiny chapel has its origins as a simple Baptist meeting place in the forest, and is reputed to be one of the earliest in Pembrokeshire, first referred to in 1667. The chapel itself was built just before the middle of the 18th century, but has since become disused and is now a partly roofless ruin. Sadly it is in a dangerous condition, and you should not attempt to enter, but the painted plasterwork that once decorated the chancel can be glimpsed through the windows.

Retrace your steps from the stile down to the last junction and turn right, the path again quite muddy but shortly leading you to a gate. Keep going a little further to a crossing, where you should go right, the way winding on through the trees and eventually emerging through a barrier onto a broad forest track. Cross diagonally left to another barriered route, waymarked for cycles, which cuts a long, gentle descent above a wooded valley. Where the cycleway later abruptly swings to the right, keep ahead, dropping to meet another broad track at the bottom. Continue with it downhill, but some 20yd before reaching a ford go left along a path set between earthen banks.

The hilltop fort, Cilfoden Camp, is of Iron Age origin and one of several in the area. Although much overgrown by trees and scrub, its concentric defensive ditches and embankments remain a prominent feature, enclosing a quite substantial area of level ground on the summit. Another hill-fort, a mile to the south at Molleston, has been possibly identified as Gorsedd Arberth, where (according to a folk tale contained in the Mabinogion) the Lord of Dyfed, Pwyll, caught site of the enchanting Princess Rhiannon riding a white horse. Charmed by her great beauty, he set off after her, but go as fast as he might whilst her horse appeared only to walk slowly, he could not catch up with her. His fortunes later changed, however, and in true fairy story style, he made her his wife.

The path climbs away through woodland heath, shortly curving left as it is joined by another path. The hill ahead is the site of a prehistoric fort, the trail winding around the base of its southern flank; although much overgrown, the banked defences remain an impressive monument to their long-forgotten builders. Originally the ditches would have been much deeper and the banks far higher, rendered even more formidable by the addition of a wooden palisade along the top; considering the large area enclosed, it suggests a place of some importance. The path rises beside it to continue above the northern perimeter of the forest, where a more open aspect affords a splendid view to the Preseli Hills. The path curves past a junction, eventually meandering around to end at a crossing of forest roads. That to the right winds back through the trees and in due course meets the main highway at the point where you first entered this half of the forest.

To return to Blackpool Mill, cross over and carry on along the track opposite through the western part of the wood, ultimately picking up your outward route back to the car park.

WALK 31
Llawhaden

Start	Llawhaden (SN070173)
Distance	6.5 miles (10.5km)
Time	3.25hr
Height gain	1100ft (335m)
OS map	Explorer OL 36 South Pembrokeshire
Parking	Parking at eastern end of village by castle entrance
Route features	Field and woodland tracks
Public transport	Bus service to Llawhaden
Refreshments	Tearoom by Llawhaden Castle
Toilets	None

Llawhaden, where the walk begins, has been an important place since antiquity, for the hill just to the north is the site of an impressively positioned hillfort. Overlooking the river crossing at Llawhaden is a medieval castle, and at the other end of the village a stone corbel-roofed chapel survives from a hostel that was established to care for needy pilgrims on their way to St David's.

This splendid ramble explores the higher valley of the Eastern Cleddau below its junction with the Afon Syfynwy at the tiny hamlet of Gelli.

From the parking area below the castle, follow the main street west into the village, passing a public telephone box in the centre. The route leaves along the bridleway signed off on the right just beyond, but for the moment keep ahead to the far end of the village, where you will find the ruins of a medieval chapel and hospital on the left behind the village hall.

Under the protection of the castle, Llawhaden developed as an important township during the medieval period, with a weekly market and two annual fairs bringing considerable trade. Its prosperity was helped by the many pilgrims passing through on their way to St David's, and Bishop Bek (who had a large hand in the reconstruction of the castle – see below) built a rest house where they could seek food, shelter and rest. For most penitents, the pilgrimage to St David's required a long and arduous journey on foot and, perhaps with little money and the ever-attendant dangers of robbers, sickness or just simple weariness, most would have been glad of the hospitality offered. The hospital provided temporal and spiritual care, and the chapel – the only part of the complex still standing – was integral to its work. Travellers would give thanks for their safe arrival and pray for the strength necessary to complete their mission, whilst the sick would attend the daily offices as part of the curative process.

Now return to follow the bridleway beside the telephone box, signed to Holgan Camp. Go forward where it shortly forks by a small pumping station, the way narrowing beyond a cottage and dropping to cross a stream. Once over, turn off right, and continue through a gate on a pleasant path across the hillside, in spring and summer ablaze with the bright yellow flowers of broom and gorse. Where the path later splits, keep left to retain the higher ground, from where there is a fine view across the valley. As the way then curves around the side of the hill, look out for a path doubling back to the left, which first rises around the flank before making a direct assault on the summit, the site of Holgan Camp.

There are a number of hillforts in the area, but none has a better position than Holgan Camp.

Built on a spur created by the meeting of two smaller side valleys and overlooking the main valley of the Eastern Cleddau, it is protected on three sides by steep natural slopes, leaving only the western flank on which earthworks were necessary. An ancient site, it might have been occupied during the Bronze Age, as early as 2000BC, and remained in use until the Romans settled in Britain.

The hillside below Holgan Fort is covered in gorse

Go back down to the main path and continue around the hillside, eventually emerging onto a lane. Cross to a bridleway opposite, which drops across a steep, forested hillside to a farm, Dan-y-Coed. Through the farmyard, carry on along the main track up the valley above lush meadows that border the Eastern Cleddau. Eventually the way turns through a gate into the trees, later winding around to a junction of tracks beside a stream. Briefly follow it to the right before swinging away to leave the wood by Gelli Bridge.

> With a fine 18th-century chapel and an unusual fire station (but regretfully no inn or tearoom) Gelli was one of the many places along the river where woollen mills were sited. That at Gelli was later converted to steam, and at its peak operated over 16 weaving looms.

The graceful two-arched bridge spans not the Eastern Cleddau but its tributary the Afon Syfynwy, the lane beyond heading upstream alongside the main river to a junction beneath the railway. Go right to cross the Eastern Cleddau and climb the hill, leaving towards the top over a stile by a gate on the right. Follow the boundary away into the next field, cutting across about halfway along to a stile in the lower, far corner. Continue your descent beside a banking that masks a quarry excavation and, entering a wood at the bottom, go left and then right through the trees to reach the river. Sometimes through undulating woodland, sometimes at the edge of green pastures, the onward way winds downstream, eventually passing Llawhaden Church on the opposite bank. Leaving the final meadow onto a lane, cross Llawhaden Bridge and turn right along a quiet lane to the church.

> Llawhaden takes its name from the dedication of the church, St Aidan, who is thought to have been a follower of St David and came to Wales from the Celtic communities in Ireland. Although of an early foundation, much of the church is relatively

modern due to its almost complete rebuilding in the Victorian period. Some early features, however, have survived within the church, including low arches on the south side of the chancel and an ancient font. An unusual feature is the bold and almost detached tower, part of which survives from the earlier building. Another prized possession is a carved stone set into the outside wall at the east end. Dating from the 11th or 12th centuries, and sadly now so worn as to be hardly discernible, it portrays a Latin cross and circle.

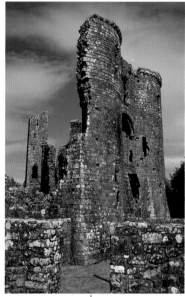

Llawhaden Castle

Just beyond the entrance to the church, turn sharp left off the lane onto a path that doubles back steeply up the hill into the village. It emerges onto the end of a street, with the castle to the right and the car park along to the left.

Possibly pre-dated by an Iron Age fort, Llawhaden's castle was founded by Bernard, the first Norman Bishop of St David's, around 1120. Razed by the Welsh in 1193, Bishop Bek began the process of rebuilding, which continued into the 14th century. It culminated in imposing defences surrounding a grand residence that rivalled the comfort of the palaces at St David's and Lamphrey, and from which the bishops could administer their estates and entertain in fitting style their royal and other guests.

WALK 32
Great Treffgarne Mountain

Start	Nant-y-coy Mill, Treffgarne (SM956252)
Distance	4.5 miles (7.2km)
Time	2.25hr
Height gain	635ft (195m)
OS map	Explorer OL 35 North Pembrokeshire
Parking	Roadside lay-by
Route features	Field and woodland paths, some moderate ascents
Public transport	Bus service past Nant-y-coy Mill
Refreshments	Tearoom at Nant-y-coy Mill
Toilets	For patrons of Nant-y-coy Mill

The rolling hills to the west of Treffgarne are a complete contrast to the abrupt gash of the Treffgarne Gorge (see Walk 33), and offer pleasant views across the Pembrokeshire countryside.

First climbing above one side of the Nant-y-coy Valley, the walk then crosses the brook upstream to complete the circuit over a broad, rounded hill, rather presumptuously entitled Great Treffgarne Mountain. However, there is nothing inconsequential about the outcrops of rock that erupt from its eastern spur, which would do credit to any mountain summit.

Follow the main road north from the mill for about 400yd to a pull-in, there doubling back sharp left on an initially metalled track to West Ford Farm. Winding round, it rises along the Nant-y-coy Valley and offers a splendid panorama to the rocky spurs bursting from the hillside at the eastern end of Great Treffgarne Mountain, and past which the ramble ultimately leads. At West Ford Farm, walk past the buildings and leave along a track through the left-hand one of a pair of more or less adjacent gates.

Quit the track where it shortly splits, entering the field between the two ways. Climb diagonally out of the corner, making for a large patch of yellow-spiked gorse at the top of the hill. The gorse marks the outline of a circular ditch and embankment defence that enclosed a prehistoric settlement, its original entrance still obvious around to the right. Walk past the earthwork to the far-left corner of the field, where you should ignore the obvious gate in favour of a stile. Go over a second stile to the left and then carry on across the fields with the hedge boundary on your left. Emerging onto a lateral track, cross to a gate and stile opposite and continue as before, the way developing in the subsequent field as a hedged track and ultimately ending at a T-junction.

Follow the broad stony track into the valley, but instead of remaining with it as it swings through a gate at the bottom carry on ahead a little further to a stile below a sycamore tree. A path then winds through an open copse to a brook, turning to follow it upstream to a stile where a

Spectacular outcrops break the skyline

161

Maiden Castle

clapper bridge and plank causeway conduct you dry-shod across the water. In the meadow beyond, head out to a gate on the far side, just left of a house, then swing right and left past its outlying barns to leave along an uphill track.

Beyond the top, the track drops to a junction where you should turn off onto a farm track. However, a short way along, leave over a stile on the right and bear left to meet the corner of a fence. Follow the boundary along the shallow crest of the hill, from where there is an excellent view south across Pembrokeshire to distant Milford Haven. Further on an equally fine panorama opens up to the Preseli Hills in the north, but more commanding of your attention is the stark outcrop of Poll Carn, lying dead ahead. Keep going by the hedge over successive stiles, shortly entering the field adjacent to Poll Carn. Now strike out to the far-left corner and, over a stile just to its right, carry on across rough heath past the left buttress of the next prominence, Maiden Castle. Maintain your direction as you drop beyond the rocks to reach a stile.

The impressively jagged crags breaking the hillside are formed from some of the oldest and hardest rocks in the country, and date to a volcanic pre-Cambrian period, over 1000 million years ago. Each cluster suggests a fortress, but the impregnability of Great Treffgarne is emphasised by its position overlooking the abrupt sides of the gorge, which rendered it ideally defensible whilst at the same time commanding control over passage through the cleft below. Settlers during the Iron Age took advantage of its qualities, constructing ditched embankments around its western flank.

Over that – and still losing height – carry on ahead until you reach a waymark. Go right to a crossing path and there turn left, very soon passing a permissive path that doubles back to the final outcrop, Great Treffgarne Rocks. The way back, however, continues along the path ahead, following the lane at its end down the hill to Nant-y-coy Mill.

163

WALK 33
Treffgarne Gorge

Start	Nant-y-coy Mill, Treffgarne (SM956252)
Distance	4.25 miles (6.8km)
Time	2.25hr
Height gain	675ft (205m)
OS map	Explorer OL 35 North Pembrokeshire
Parking	Roadside lay-by
Route features	Field and woodland paths, some moderate ascents
Public transport	Bus service past Nant-y-coy Mill
Refreshments	Tearoom at Nant-y-coy Mill
Toilets	For patrons of Nant-y-coy Mill

Below Wolf's Castle the Western Cleddau falls through a deep, wooded gorge, which appears quite at odds against the gently rolling hills of the surrounding countryside.

The walk starts near the northern end of the gorge at Nant-y-coy, once a woollen mill, and follows a path above the western slope, from which there are fine views across the ravine. Your return is through the mixed woodland that cloaks the steep eastern side, where the trees conceal an abortive 19th-century attempt to bring a railway through the valley.

Begin along a narrow lane that climbs determinedly away from the main road, just lower down from the mill. After the steepest pull – and where the public road ends by a small parking area – leave along a waymarked footpath on the left, then bear left at an immediate fork to rise comfortably across the open bracken heath. Not far along a permissive path branches off to Great Treffgarne Rocks over on the left, winding through the bank-and-ditch fortifications of a prehistoric fort that once commanded the narrow valley below (see Walk 32).

Treffgarne Gorge cuts through some of the oldest rocks in the country, created around 1000 million years ago when cataclysmic volcanoes spewed unimaginable quantities of lava out of the earth.

The cooling lava formed a very hard rock, which the uplifting and erosion of later deposits has again laid bare at the surface. A couple of theories have been proposed as to how the gorge was cut. One suggests it was due to water escaping from a vast lake that had built up when northward-flowing rivers were blocked by a frozen Irish Sea, whilst the other argues that it was scoured by waters released from melting glaciers as the ice age drew to a close.

There is a splendid view from the outcrop across the valley to Little Treffgarne Rocks, whilst to the south lie the craggy prominences of Maiden Castle, the more distant Poll Carn, and the shallow cresting summit ridge of Treffgarne Mountain running west from them. Seen from here, the rocks of Maiden Castle are the most impressive for their grotesque shape, but the other crags generate their own interest with changing angles as you walk on.

The view along Treffgarne Gorge

165

Return to the main path and continue along it to the left, passing through a couple of gates before leaving the rough heath behind. Keep ahead across a pasture to the second of two gates at the far side, and follow a track to Mount Pleasant Farm. Depart along its access road, which emerges onto the corner of a lane, and walk downhill past St Michael's Church to the main road at the bottom.

Take advantage of its bridge to cross the Western Cleddau, but then turn off onto a quiet lane signed to Spittal. Initially running beside a small stream, it enters a tunnel-like bridge, piercing a skewed embankment on which the Fishguard railway traverses the valley. At the far side, bear left at a fork below a Baptist chapel and continue at the edge of a species-rich, waterlogged wood. Nearing some cottages, where the lane again forks, keep left once more, but at the entrance to Millbrook Lodge, veer right. After crossing a stream and passing the gated entrance to stables, the track rises behind in a steep curve, gaining height along the wooded valley side. Approaching the gates of Hazel Grove higher up, leave through a kissing gate to follow an obvious path through the trees, keeping ahead at a waymarked split, just further along. The dense leaf cover allows little scope for flowers, but for a brief period in spring bluebells carpet the ground in a flurry of delicate blue. Shortly the way crosses a stile into a plantation of conifers, returning to deciduous woodland beyond a stream. In time the way begins to lose height, sometimes quite steeply, and eventually descends steps to a fork. ◀

You can marginally shorten the walk here by dropping to the river, where a bridge above a low cataract enables you to reach the main road, the Nant-y-coy Mill lying 0.5 mile (800m) to the right.

Even if you are completing the full circuit – and not taking the short cut – the view beside the river is quite enchanting and worth the effort of the brief deviation. On the way down, the path crosses a level overgrown track, a relic of Brunel's ill-fated project.

Return to the junction and climb the other path, which rises fairly steeply before turning along the top edge of the wood. Carry on, crossing a stile and later a stream, prior to emerging into a small grassy clearing. At this point bear left off the main path (which would otherwise climb around to Treffgarne Farm) in favour of a vague trod into

BRUNEL'S RAILWAY PLANS

Almost hidden by the trees, the terrace cut into the hard rock of the precipitously steep valley side is a relic of Brunel's unsuccessful endeavour during the 1840s to force his broad-gauge railway through the gorge. He brought the line from Swansea, intending it to connect with an Irish ferry terminus, at that time proposed for Fishguard. However, the incredibly hard pre-Cambrian rocks proved too much for the engineers, and bankrupted the firm. In the end the notion of a port on the north coast was abandoned and Brunel switched his attention to Milford Haven, constructing a port and new town at Neyland. It was another 60 years before the railway finally came through Treffgarne.

the trees beyond, losing a little height to cross a stream and then a stile. To the right of the stile a clearer path continues ahead through a timber plantation.

Breaking out at the far side there is a fine view across the valley to Wolf's Castle as the way passes Little Treffgarne Rocks. Entering a denser plantation the path descends and then suddenly regains the open hillside once more. Continue obliquely downwards to a stile, over which make for a bridge beneath the railway embankment. Cross the field beyond to a footbridge spanning the river, and climb around left to reach the main road. Turn left and walk back to the mill.

Great Treffgarne Rocks

WALK 34
Llys-y-frân Reservoir

Start	Llys-y-frân Visitor Centre (SN040244)
Distance	6.25 miles (10.1km)
Time	3hr
Height gain	920ft (280m)
OS map	Explorer OL 35 North Pembrokeshire
Parking	Car park by Visitor Centre
Route features	Clear paths throughout
Public transport	Bus service to Visitor Centre
Refreshments	Café at Visitor Centre
Toilets	Toilets at Visitor Centre

If you want to avoid some of the uphill work on this route, yet enjoy the best corners of the park, start from the western car park and follow the path on that side, simply turning about when you have wandered far enough.

This is an easy walk leading round the Llys-y-frân Reservoir that can be undertaken on a reasonable track throughout, making it possible for pushchairs. Begin along the drive from the main entrance car park to the Visitor Centre, where signs direct you onwards towards the western car park and viewpoint. The way winds down below the foot of the dam before climbing to the car park. Nestling in the trees beneath the dam are the ruins of a cottage, Dan y Coed, birthplace of William Penfro Rowlands (1860–1937) who composed the tune 'Blaen-Wern', to which Charles Wesley's hymn 'Love Divine' is sometimes sung.

A track by toilets at the far end of the car park leads into the woodland above the lake. However, a little way along you can drop onto an alternative, narrower path at the water's edge. Later rejoining the main track keep going around the head of a small inlet, beyond which the track cuts across a meadow to continue above a steep bank overlooking another tributary arm of the lake. After dipping steeply to an inflowing stream, stick with the main track through the trees, for although paths later lead invitingly to the shore they do

The Llys-y-frân dam

not afford an ongoing route. Eventually, turning the point to rejoin the main body of the lake, a picnic area offers a splendid vantage for a grand view across the water to the dam.

The Llys-y-frân Reservoir is the largest in Pembrokeshire, and was begun in 1968 to meet ever-increasing demands for water by the rapid growth of the oil and power industries that had developed around Milford Haven. The original proposal to construct a dam 150ft (45m) high across the Afon Sŷfynwy far surpassed the needs of the time, and anticipated future industrial growth in the area. However, approval was granted only for a 110ft- (33m-) high dam, but with an option to raise the retaining wall if required. In consequence it was necessary to lay the foundations as originally designed, embedded 70ft (21m) in the bedrock. Milford Haven's anticipated continued expansion, as yet, has not been realised and

169

there is no foreseeable need to exercise the option to increase the height of the dam. However, following successive dry summers in the early 1990s, the overflow was raised by 5ft (1.5m), effectively increasing the capacity by some 15 per cent. With a greatest depth of 100ft (30m) and almost 1.5 miles (2.4km) long, the lake is a prominent feature in the Pembrokeshire countryside and an excellent resource for both leisure activities and wildlife.

The way continues along the western bank, sometimes in wood and at other times beside open fields, occasionally dipping and climbing to negotiate streams feeding into the reservoir. The lake progressively tapers towards the upper end of the valley and there the path is forced through a narrow gap in an outcrop of the Ordovician slate bedrock. Just beyond, a secluded pool is a good place to observe some of the many waterbirds that are resident here. Carry on over another stream to the head of the lake, where a bridge spans the Afon Syfynwy.

With over two-thirds of the distance and most of the undulating terrain behind you, it is now an easy stroll back to the foot of the lake. There is little to be gained by dropping from the main path to the water's edge, although a hide, signed off a short distance along,

The top of the dam

provides a sheltered halt from which to view the birds on the water. The lakeside beyond is largely unwooded, but the grassy shores attract geese and swans to distract your progress as you walk back to the car park.

A secluded pool at the top of the reservoir

Several species of small mammal live in the woodland rising above the lakeshore, including stoats, weasels, shrews and voles. However, these tend to be secretive, and thus hard to spot, but you will be unlucky not to come across a grey squirrel, or perhaps even a fox. If you walk quietly during the late evening, you might also catch sight of a badger. The lake boasts an impressive bird list, with over 140 species being recorded and more than 50 breeding here. Amongst the more everyday residents keep your eyes open for herons, moorhens and coots, as well, of course, for swans. Smaller birds include wrens, several kinds of finches, wagtails and great spotted woodpeckers. Common too is the bird from which the lake takes its name frân – the crow, and rooks, hooded crows, jackdaws and magpies are all evident in the trees around the lake. Winter is the best time to see waterbirds, and pochard, teal, goldeneye and pintail have all been recorded.

WALK 35
Rhydwilym

Start	Rhydwilym (SN114248)
Distance	3.75 miles (6km)
Time	2hr
Height gain	655ft (200m)
OS map	Explorer OL 35 North Pembrokeshire
Parking	By the village hall at Rhydwilym
Route features	Woodland and field paths with some strenuous sections
Public transport	None
Refreshments	Farm tearoom at Pencraig-fawr
Toilets	None

There are many places in Pembrokeshire where you can experience outstandingly beautiful scenery yet hardly meet a soul all day, and the upper reaches of the Eastern Cleddau is just such a spot.

Above the tiny hamlet of Rhydwilym the vale narrows to something of a gorge, for the most part cloaked in splendid mixed woodland. The route follows the line of an old track up the valley before crossing to the eastern side, where wholesale quarrying was undertaken during the 19th century. Now profusely overgrown, the silent workings are a delight for wildflower lovers.

Walk from the village hall past the church and cross a bridge over the Eastern Cleddau to carry on up the lane. A few steps beyond a turning off to Llanycefn, leave through a gate on the right and follow the field boundary away. A grass track develops, which continues over stiles beside marsh, meadow and then a young wood. Further on the way gains height and, although hardly visible, the river betrays its presence as it surges noisily over the rocks littering its bed. Occasional waymarks confirm the onward path through the gorse and broom cloaking the hillside. Emerging over a stile onto a grassy terrace, keep ahead, joining a contained track that rises to the farm at Pencraig-fawr.

The present owners welcome passers-by to their tearoom, and have undertaken considerable research into the history of the area. There was a Saxon settlement on the hillside above the farm, and pipes found in the fields suggest an even earlier occupation during Roman times. A monastic house was later established, which provided food, shelter and care for pilgrims making their way to the holy shrines at St David's Cathedral.

Walk forward through the yard, leaving by a gate at the far side into a meadow. Cut left in the next field to a gate near the top corner from which a track leads past a derelict farm. Joining another track from cottages, carry on a little further, but approaching a house turn off through a waymarked gate on the right. A path skirts the garden to enter the woodland beyond and then slopes through the trees to the base of the valley, where a narrow iron bridge spans the river.

A winding path climbs away through heaps of spoil from old quarry workings, which despite their apparent barrenness sustain a surprising variety of wildflowers. Within the space of a few steps you can find mossy saxifrage, mouse-ear hawkweed, English stonecrop, bird's-foot trefoil, heather, rock speedwell and even exquisitely sweet wild strawberries. At a crossing of tracks go right, but then take the left branch where the way shortly splits. Climbing easily away, ignore another track that branches off on the left.

The abandoned quarries were extensively worked during the 19th century to provide roofing slates for the burgeoning industrial towns and cities spawned by the steam-powered industrial revolution. Some of the stone went to roof the monumental Gothic masterpiece of the Houses of

*An iron bridge
crosses the river*

Parliament, designed by Charles Barry and
A.W.N. Pugin and begun just three years after the
Westminster Palace had been destroyed by fire in
October 1834.

As you pass through a gateway out of the quarry, turn
immediately right onto a narrow path into the trees,
which in springtime is completely overgrown with bluebells. Over a couple of streams, cross successive stiles to
gain the bottom corner of a field and climb away steeply
to a gate near the top-left corner. Through that, follow the
hedgebank away to the right, continuing in the subsequent field, but with the hedge now on your left.
Approaching the far corner, pass through a gap to the left,

but maintain your forward direction across a rough open space to join a track dropping from the left.

An old quarry track, it descends through the woodland cloaking the steep sided valley, ameliorating the gradient lower down by sharply twisting through successive zigzags. Where it abruptly ends in a marshy area beside the river, pick your way left to carry on downstream along a narrow path. A short way along a waterfall cascading down the cliff face curtains the entrance to an abandoned mine adit. It does not penetrate very far, and either the tunnellers soon abandoned their efforts, or the passage has since become choked with debris. A little further on is another curiosity, a small shelter cut into the rock. Worked facings either side of the low doorway and a flagged floor suggest a significant purpose, and it perhaps served as a hut for the tallyman, who kept account of the stone leaving the quarry.

Not far beyond, the path abruptly enters a field. Go left for 100yd to a gate and then continue on a broad track back into the trees. Where it splits, fork right, now on the 'Landsker Borderlands Trail'. When you shortly reach a field gate, instead of going through, pass to its left and follow a path around at the tree fringe. Over a stile and plank bridge, bear right at a fork, soon climbing another stile into a dense conifer plantation. Emerging at the far side of the forest, keep going across a rough pasture before ending back at Rhydwilym beside the village hall.

The tiny hamlet of Rhydwilym is dominated by a large Welsh chapel, focus of a Baptist community founded in 1668 by a small group of dissenters led by a local vicar, the Reverend William Jones. It was the first Baptist assembly to be established in west Wales, but within 10 years had grown to over 110 members. The first chapel was built here in 1701, funded by the generosity of John Evans, and during succeeding years the church was extended. The members are baptised according to their custom by total immersion in the river water, and a baptistery was built for the purpose.

WALK 36
Cwm Gwaun

Start	Cilrhedyn Bridge (SN004348)
Distance	4 miles (6.4km)
Time	2.25hr
Height gain	860ft (260m)
OS map	Explorer OL 35 North Pembrokeshire
Parking	Roadside car park by bridge
Route features	Woodland and field paths, moderate climb
Public transport	None
Refreshments	Pub at Llanychaer
Toilets	None

When we discovered this walk part was all but impassable, and the old graded quarry track through Tre-llwyn Wood overgrown. Thanks to the efforts of National Park staff (who, together with County Council rangers, have worked hard in recent years to clear many of Pembrokeshire's forgotten footpaths) it is open once again.

This idyllic ramble climbs out of Cwm Gwaun through old woodland to an abandoned church and holy well nestling in the lee of a hill above, the top of which offers a fine view down to the coast at Fishguard. The return to Cilrhedyn takes you back beside the river, passing close to the Bridge End Inn just off the trail at Llanychaer.

Follow the lane from the car park over the bridge, but turn off left as it then bends in front of a farm cottage. Through the yard, carry on along a track, which leads through a gateway and over a stream to another cottage. Pass that to the right and continue behind on a grassy path above a meadow at the fringe of trees. Beyond a couple of stiles, the way enters the meadow, leading naturally to a gate at the far end beside the river. Cross a stile to its right and follow a contained path that soon swings first to the right and then to the left, turning away from a stream it has briefly followed. Leave it at that point, delving ahead into the trees, but immediately bear right to find a terraced path that rises in a well-graded ascent along the valley side.

Emerging over a stile into a clearing at the top, walk around to the right through a gap in the gorse and bramble bushes to enter the corner of a field. Strike out past a standing stone in the middle to the far, upper corner, where there is a stile on the left, then follow the bottom hedge bank away, keeping at the edge of successive fields until you reach some barns. Joining a track that rises past them from the left, follow it on until eventually meeting a lane near a junction.

In a field beside the road (just up from the junction) is Llanllawer holy well, a stone vault protecting the source. To an unsophisticated mind, pure water issuing from the solid earth is miraculous – a gift of life from the gods. Long before the arrival of Christianity on these shores such sites were revered, places where man could commune with the spirits of the afterworld. Christianity adopted such places in the same way that it absorbed many of the Pagan feast days into its own calendar, replacing the old Mother Earth myths with tales of saintly miracles and happenings. Many wells were credited with healing or life-giving properties, a belief not always unfounded, for many of these springs have waters rich in beneficial minerals. The one at Llanllawer was said to ease complaints of the eyes, and the inflicted would undergo total immersion in the water, a remembrance of Christ's baptism by John.

Wells also became the focus of pilgrimage, either in their own right or as stopping points along the road (in this instance to St David's), a custom that lasted throughout the medieval period up to the Reformation, when such practices were banned. But changes of law have always been notoriously ineffective in altering belief or attitude, and such sites continued to be visited, in this case to the present day, as the prayer rags, flowers and other offerings around it attest. Sadly the neighbouring church has fared less well and is quickly falling into a state of dangerous disrepair, visited now only by a pair of barn owls. A curious feature, however, is a primitive carving exposed in the rendering high on the south wall, which depicts a circle quartered by a cross with a spot cut into the middle of each segment, and is said to be a representation of the ichthys.

The holy well at Llanllawer

Cross to a gate facing the junction and follow the field edge past a derelict church. Beyond, bear right to climb over the hill, where a view suddenly opens ahead to Goodwick Harbour. At the far corner the field narrows to a track that falls to a gate. Instead of going through it, turn left and drop through another gate to come out at a farm.

Go forward across a tarmac track to a yard in front of the farmhouse, and then swing right at a waymark beside a stone barn to pass through a gate. A few steps further on turn left through another gate into a field and briefly follow the left boundary to a waymark. Now cut across to a stile at the bottom of the field, from which a path descends left into a wood. Meeting a crossing path go left, then drop steeply to the Afon Gwaun, following it upstream to a bridge. Remain on this bank and carry on up the valley, the woodland shortly giving way to a swathe of neglected water meadow. Beyond, the woodland quietly closes in again, and an old track leads onwards to a lane.

The Gwaun Valley might be regarded as a window back through time in more ways than one. Reached only by a narrow road and occupied by little more than a handful of families, it is a wonderful escape from the hectic bustle of our modern world. Its rich woodlands hark back to the native forest that once covered the area and support an immensely varied and abundant flora and fauna, whilst the manner in which the narrow strip of land along its base is farmed perhaps acknowledges traditional attitudes more so than many places.

Another curious oddity is that the inhabitants continue to celebrate the Julian New Year, which now falls on 13 January. The difference arises because under the old calendar every centennial year was a leap year, on average fractionally longer than the astronomical year. By 1582 the discrepancy amounted to 10 days and Pope

At the edge of Tre-llwyn Wood

If you want refreshment, follow the lane over the river to the Bridge End Inn.

Gregory issued a decree losing the days between 5 and 15 October and in future having only every fourth centennial year a leap year. The new calendar was only gradually adopted throughout Europe, and by the time Britain changed in 1752 the difference had increased to 11 days. The festival is something of an occasion in the valley, with a sumptuous feast, gifts for the children and, of course a spirited celebration in the pub. ◀

To continue the walk, go left to a bend, leaving there to resume the riverside path. Later emerging into a meadow, bear left around its edge, returning to the wood further on. Beyond a stile, the way continues as a fenced path, eventually joining your outward route. Keep ahead as you enter a meadow over a stile, but then remember to climb left to a second stile after about 100yd, as you retrace your steps to Cilrhedyn Bridge.

WALK 37
Coed Clŷn and Coed Kilkiffeth

Start	Cilrhedyn Bridge (SN004348)
Distance	1.75 miles (2.8km)
Time	1.25hr
Height gain	640ft (195m)
OS map	Explorer OL 35 North Pembrokeshire
Parking	Roadside car park by bridge
Route features	Woodland and field paths, moderate climb
Public transport	None
Refreshments	None
Toilets	None

Although there is a bit of a stiff pull through forest plantation at the beginning of this short walk, the way lies along a broad track and the climb is soon accomplished. The route continues through more natural woodland and then eventually drops to amble back along the bottom of the valley.

There is a delightful picnic area beside the car park and, if you are looking for a relaxing end to the day, it is an ideal quiet place to unwind.

A broad timber track climbs steeply away behind the car park, turning to adopt a more gentle gradient as it continues along the forested valley side. Towards the top, look for an adit cut into the many-layered shale rock on the right. With its purpose now lost in time, we can only speculate as to why it was dug; perhaps a prospector's tunnel sunk in search of useful ore, or alternatively a small quarry to reach unweathered slate. Beyond a bend a little further on the track ends abruptly in a side valley. Go left across a stream, turn up beside it for some 20yd, then double back left to undulate through a conifer plantation, high above the main valley.

Cwm Gwaun above Pontfaen

The conifers growing in Clŷn Wood are a commercial crop and, being closely spaced, allow little light to penetrate to the ground at any time of the year. Their needle-like leaves provide hardly any nutrient return to the soil, thus very few plants can grow amongst them and, with so little food, there is not much wildlife either. However, such trees form only a small proportion of the woodland in the valley and in the naturally regenerating areas encountered later on the picture is very different. There many kinds of trees grow together – oak, ash, rowan and holly – and their haphazard distribution creates small clearings where the sun can flood in. The woodland floor too is not barren; in contrast to areas where sycamore predominates, the leaves of these trees are generally small and allow sufficient light to filter through for year-round growth. The falling autumn foliage quickly rots, adding to the rich underbed of humus and encouraging a tremendous diversity of wildflowers, such as bluebells, primroses, violets and lesser celandine. More woody plants such as ivy and bramble abound as well and nectar, berries, nuts and seeds attract a range of insects, birds and small mammals.

The path soon breaks from the trees onto a bracken and scrub heath, where there is a view across to the Carn Ingli ridge. Before long the trail begins to fall, weaving through bushes and then re-entering the wood below. Lower down, at a junction by the bottom corner of the conifer plantation, go right, twisting into the base of the valley. Heading back downstream, the path eventually rises to rejoin the outward track. Instead of remaining with it to its end, however, you can leave a little further on at a waymark, where a stepped path drops to a meadow and picnic area beside the car park.

Kilkiffeth Wood

WALK 38
Coed Pontfaen

Start	Pontfaen (SN024339)
Distance	3 miles (4.8km)
Time	1.5hr
Height gain	570ft (175m)
OS map	Explorer OL 35 North Pembrokeshire
Parking	Roadside car park
Route features	Woodland walk, gentle climbs
Public transport	None
Refreshments	Dyffryn Arms (across the bridge) does not serve food, but has a reputation for good beer, which comes straight from the barrel in time-honoured fashion
Toilets	None

Although beginning with a bit of a pull, this walk is not strenuous, and wanders through the woodland and forest cloaking the higher reaches of Cwm Gwaun. Its conclusion lies along the base of the valley although not always by the river, which wanders sinuously through the marshy meadows covering the dale's almost flat bottom.

From the car park, follow the lane away from the bridge up a steep wooded bank.

Just beyond the point at which you leave the lane is the tiny church of Pontfaen. It is dedicated to St Brynach, a 6th-century Irish hermit monk who built the first church here before moving on to establish a small monastery near Nevern. Legends give two reasons for his leaving: one that he was chased away by evil spirits, and another that an angel told him to carry on wandering until he came across a place where he found a white sow with her piglets.

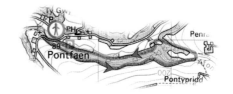

Around a bend at the top, double back left onto a waymarked track, which undulates along the top fringe of the almost precipitous valley side. Occasional glimpses through the dense mantle of trees reveal the river meandering within a strip of flat, lush meadow below. Keep ahead at a fork and again much further on, where a route is waymarked down into the valley. Eventually the path begins a steady descent, passing several tunnel entrances of an extensive badger sett. Shortly dropping more sharply, the way twists to a foot-bridge spanning the Afon Cwmau.

The Gwaun Valley is a product of the last ice age, a deep, steep-sided valley cleaving away a shoulder from the Preseli Hills. It was caused by the run-off of unimaginable amounts of water released as the

The Afon Gwaun above Pontfaen

185

immense ice sheets, which overlay the Preseli Hills at a depth of up to 1000ft (305m), melted in the face of a warming climate. Being so declivitous – almost sheer in places – the valley sides escaped clearance and cultivation and their woodland covering is a remnant of the ancient forests that once spread over the whole area.

However, it has not remained untouched, for it has provided a constant source of wood throughout the centuries. Careful coppicing and limited felling has promoted continuous regeneration of the native woodland, and with it the smaller plants and flowers that make up the undergrowth. Amongst the indigenous trees you will find oak, hazel, rowan, ash, birch and holly, whilst the carpet below harbours foxglove, herb robert and bluebell at different times of the year. There is an amazingly luxuriant growth of ferns, mosses and lichens, encouraged by the damp, dark conditions prevailing in the shade of the trees. Keep your eyes open for animals and birds as you wander through the woods. Badger setts, marked by prodigious tunnels and often accompanied by signs of recent excavation, abound, and although you might not see one, the presence of a fox is often revealed by the musty scent left by the males to mark out their territories. If you are very lucky, you might even see an otter in the river.

Cross to a bridleway above the far bank and follow it down to the left. Where a track later climbs to join it keep ahead, in due course dropping to a junction at the bottom. A short distance to the left, a footbridge provides a dry-shod crossing of the river, taking you on towards a small farm. However, almost immediately go over a stile, from which a path then rises around the rear of the buildings and leads to a three-way signpost. Keep right and continue through the wood at the base of the valley, ultimately returning to the car park at Pontfaen.

WALK 39
Mynydd Caregog and Carn Ingli

Start	Sychbant (SN045350)
Distance	7 miles (11.3km)
Time	4hr
Height gain	1410ft (430m)
OS map	Explorer OL 35 North Pembrokeshire
Parking	Parking area and picnic site at Sychbant
Route features	Moorland hill paths and woodland tracks; an initial steep climb
Public transport	None
Refreshments	Tearoom at nearby Penlan-Uchaf Gardens
Toilets	Adjacent to car park

After a steep but short climb from the valley, the way leads through a commercial forest plantation which, since its acquisition by the National Park, is being progressively felled and allowed to regenerate as native woodland heath. The return into the valley is along a delightful ancient track, after which you can wander back through the woodland beside the marshy gathering grounds of the Afon Gwaun, or alternatively take a somewhat shorter route along the quiet lane.

A waymarked path from the left-hand rear corner of the car park crosses a stream above the picnic area to a gate. Turn right and climb steeply up the bracken and open wood of the valley side, keeping ahead at a junction and then swinging right to recross the stream. Further up the gradient eases, passing a path into the private grounds of a Christian retreat.

Ffald-y-Brenin, 'the sheepfold of the King', was the realisation in 1984 of a vision given to its founders Phyllida and Peter Mould. Non-denominational, but reflecting Christian values and practising a

Note Inexperienced walkers may find navigation difficult in poor weather or visibility.

There are shorter routes onto Carningli Common, but we feel this is the most rewarding, combining the secretive beauties of Cwm Gwaun and splendid, open heather moorland with the breath-taking ruggedness of Carn Ingli.

simple lifestyle, the retreat offers a tranquil and unsullied environment in which to reflect, pray and appreciate the serene beauty of the valley. They welcome visitors to share its quiet peace and enjoy the stunning views.

Carry on to a gate at the top, which opens into the Penlan Forest. Now owned by the National Park, the monotonous ranks of conifers are being harvested, and in time a more natural woodland heath will spread across the hillside. Initially following the boundary to the right, the path later cuts across the former plantation, where occasional markers ensure that the way is in no doubt. After passing a junction, the trail later curves left, eventually leaving the forest to continue as a track.

Emerging onto a lane, walk up to a parking area by the crest of the hill and go right again. An obvious track leads across a gorse and heather moor, which in summer dons an imperial purple hue flecked with splashes of brilliant yellow, and hums as countless bees flit between the flowers. Meeting the far top corner of the Penlan Forest, turn left and walk up to the next fence corner and go right, the path still a clear swathe through the heath.

The marked permissive path continues in a gentle arc across the hillside towards the spectacular eruption of rocks at the eastern end of the Carn Ingli hill. However, as you pass a stile from which a path drops to the right past another imposing outcrop, Carn Edward, an informal path swings off to the high point

of Carningli Common. From there you can strike across to Carn Ingli itself, picking your way through the jumble of boulders and slabs that crowd its western flank to reach the summit.

View from Carn Ingli to Newport

Hilltops and mountain summits are imbued with a special attraction, but Carn Ingli has a greater sense of mystery about it than most. Perhaps the startling jagged prominence of the crag suggested the abode of an awesome god to the ancient peoples who lived around its flanks, or its lofty separateness from the lush valleys made it a place to commune with the spirits. Stories associate the site with the 6th-century Irish monk St Brynach, relating that he lived there as a hilltop hermit for a while before building his reclusive monastery beside the Afon Gamman near present-day Nevern. The translation of 'Carn Ingli' as the 'hill of angels' lends some credence to the notion, but others interpret it as meaning simply the 'cairn of the chieftain Ingli'.

189

Whatever, Carn Ingli has lost nothing of its singular appeal, whether for the spectacular views from its summit or, as some believe, the special reverence it commands from its positioning upon a ley line. The place had real significance for the early inhabitants of the area, for the whole hilltop is dotted with the remains of settlement. Many separate hut sites have been identified, small circular or annular heaps of stones, often with the doorway still identifiable. The low stone walls would have been roofed over using wood and thatch, with an entrance passage turned away from the prevailing wind. Vague traces of field enclosures can be made out surrounding the settlement area, the upland climate then being more suitable for agriculture than today.

The cliffs have the appearance of castle walls, and they once served that purpose, a defensible refuge against pillaging forays by neighbouring clans. The natural buttresses were a formidable defence in themselves, but the remains of drystone rampart walls can still be seen in the heather and bracken surrounding the hill. Archaeological investigations suggest that the settlement was established around AD300 and remained in more or less continuous use for the next 800 years.

Make your way along the rocky top to the northern end of the crags, where a cairn marks the start of a path down to the right. Initially falling quite steeply, it passes through the stony barrier of a prehistoric defence. Go forward over a lateral path, dropping between a pair of pillars and on down a disused tramway that served to lower stone cut from a quarry in the rock behind. At another crossing track, veer right, shortly joining a narrow lane, which becomes a gravel track beyond a farm. Continue past another farm and later, a junction, the way subsequently narrowing as it descends through woodland. Keep ahead to another farm at the bottom, exiting through the yard onto the sharp bend of a lane. ◀

To shorten the walk, merely follow the lane right back to the parking area at Sychbant.

Heather moor on Mynydd Caregog

To continue, cross the valley, then abandon the lane through a right-hand gate on the next bend. A path winds at the edge of Coed Gelli-fawr above a marsh, eventually passing the ruins of a farm. At a fork, bear right, signed 'Tregynon', and drop past the scant remains of a mill to cross a bridge. Winding round to follow the flow, stay ahead at a junction and carry on to a stile. The path drops to a stream and then appears to swing left, but instead cross it to emerge in a clearing. Now walk forward, ford another stream, and re-enter the woods. Mounting a stile, keep going amongst the trees, later passing another ruined farm. Not far beyond, look for a stile on the right, from which a path is signed off to Sychbant. After crossing the river, turn right along the lane back to the car park.

WALK 40
Pentre Evan Nature Reserve

Start	Pentre Evan (SN092383)
Distance	5.25 miles (8.4km)
Time	2.5hr
Height gain	730ft (225m)
OS map	Explorer OL 35 North Pembrokeshire
Parking	Roadside car park
Route features	Woodland and field paths
Public transport	None
Refreshments	None
Toilets	None

The Afon Nyfer valley woodlands are now designated as a nature reserve, a splendid place to explore, and providing one of the contrasting aspects of this delightful walk.

Below the Preseli's northern foothills and overlooking the valley of the Afon Nyfer is one of the finest native woodlands remaining in the county. Once through the trees, the route of this walk leads onto the high ground above, where stark outcrops of rock mirror those on the wilder mountains lying just to the south. The return is past Pentre Ifan, the most outstanding of the many cromlechs that dot the Pembrokeshire landscape.

Walk down the drive from the car park towards Pentre Evan, bearing right at a fork to pass around the buildings. After a few steps, turn off through a gate on the right and head half-left to a stile on the far side at the edge of a wood. A winding path leads away to the right, crossing more stiles and eventually reaching a lane by a bridge.

The Pentre Evan Nature Reserve encompasses a tract of woodland that dates from at least the 12th century. However, it has not been left to its own devices for the last 800 years, but carefully managed to produce a steady supply of timber. Although mature oaks and other substantial trees would occasionally be felled to provide large beams for construction, shipbuilding and wagon frames, a more regular harvest was achieved by coppicing. Periodic cutting back to a bole produced small timber, typically of ash and hazel, but also of oak and other species too. Such poles were ideal for making furniture, fences and tools, and for charcoal burning, with the debris providing domestic fuel. The shelter gave winter grazing for pigs and cattle and also, no doubt, some game for the table. This sustainable local economy was unsuited to the demands of modern industry, and in the 1960s much of the area was replanted with quick-growing conifers, destroying the diversity of wildlife habitats. Happily, thinking has now changed, and as the softwood is felled the land is being left to regenerate with native species. As traditional methods are reintroduced, the woodland is slowly regaining its former richness.

Immediately over the bridge, turn back into the wood along a narrowing green track that winds to the right. Beyond a gate, the path leads to a crossing, where you should go right. Bear right again at a later fork and carry on near the edge of the wood. Keep ahead when you meet a crossing gravel track, but then just before reaching a barrier, look for a gate on the right into the adjacent Tycanol Nature Reserve.

The reserve here extends to moorland and pasture, and the woodland has not been disturbed by wholesale felling. As a result there is a range of different habitats that include flower-rich grazing and damp woodlands prolific in ferns, mosses and fungi, with over a quarter of all British species of lichen being found in this small area.

Carnedd Meibion-Owen

An old sunken track climbs gently away beside an open heath. Where it then forks, walk forward through a gate, rising between ancient twisted trees, their boles – like the outcropping rocks and boulders littering the woodland floor – smothered beneath a thick, soft carpet of mosses and lichens. Carry on to another fork, and there go right to find a ladder stile beside a gate. Keep going at the edge of more open woodland, eventually crossing another ladder stile to arrive at a track.

Turn right, still near the edge of the wood, the way softening to a grassy drove and shortly leading towards a gate. Just before reaching it, bear left into the trees at a waymark, cross an old wall and then go right. The path winds through more moss-encrusted outcrops and boulders and soon leads to a stile at the edge of the reserve. Instead of crossing, double back left over a bracken heath to climb beside a wooded valley. Drifting to the opposite slope part-way up, carry on to the top of the rise, passing a junction to continue at the base of a wooded slope. In a little while meeting an old grass track, double back obliquely up the bank, breaking out through bracken to a gate at the top. The way continues by a wall over the top of an open hill past a series of rugged rocky outcrops, then drops to a stile. To the left, a broad track leads downhill to the corner of a lane. Keep ahead and, before long, you will see the entrance to the Pentre Ifan burial chamber.

Erected some 5500 years ago during the Neolithic Age, the Pentre Ifan tomb is one of the most spectacular prehistoric sites in Pembrokeshire. Supported on only three points and weighing some 16 tons, the massive 17ft (5m) capstone forms a roof for a chamber that would have been buried beneath a mound of stones, the whole monument being around 120ft (37m) long. The entrance lay through a portal situated at the southern end (to the left as you approach from the lane), laboriously reopened and closed every time a new interment was made. Although the grave would

Pentre Ifan burial chamber

have been used over a long period of time and no doubt contained the relics of many successive generations of chieftains and other important members of the clan, archaeological excavation revealed only a few pieces of pottery and some flint tools.

Continue down the hill for a further 0.25 mile (400m) to a right-hand bend. Pass through the second of two gates on the left, and follow the field edge away from the lane. Reaching a track at the far side, cross to the right-hand one of two gates opposite and carry on across the next field. Over a stile go left, and remain by the left-hand edge in the subsequent field. Follow the curve around at the far end, looking for a waymark denoting a path into the trees.

Over a stile and stream, walk ahead into the wood, later turning right at the second path off. After passing a small pool, go left at a junction, shortly meeting a broader track. To the right, beyond a stream, it leads to Pentre Evan, circling the buildings to the left before climbing back to the car park.

WALK 41

Cilgerran and the Teifi Marshes
Nature Reserve

Start	Teifi Marshes Nature Reserve (SN186449)
Distance	3.5 miles (5.6km)
Time	1.5hr
Height gain	400ft (120m)
OS map	Explorer OL 35 North Pembrokeshire
Parking	Nature Reserve car park (pay and display)
Route features	Woodland and riverside paths, sometimes demanding strenuous walking; a short section of the gorge path may be impassable after exceptional rain
Public transport	Bus service to Cilgerran (alternative start)
Refreshments	Café at Visitor Centre, pub and tearoom in Cilgerran
Toilets	At Visitor Centre and in Cilgerran

Managed by the Dyfed Wildlife Trust, the Teifi Marsh Nature Reserve covers some 350 acres (141ha) and incorporates three very different types of environment: an extensive marsh at the foot of the Teifi Gorge; ancient mixed woodland; and, of course, the river itself. It is a great place to spend a day and an ideal starting point for a splendid walk that follows the river upstream to the old market town of Cilgerran. Under the protection of an imposing castle, its importance grew during the medieval period for, being at the tidal limit, it was the highest point to which seagoing boats could sail. The way back lies through a strip of woodland, where native oak and ash are remnants of the ancient forest that once cloaked the whole hillside.

The walk begins from the Visitor Centre, where a path signed as the 'Otter Trail' heads towards a viewpoint above the river. There is a good outlook to Cardigan over the marsh, wet scrubby woodland lapped by the tides, regarded as one of the finest examples of its type in the

There are several places in Pembrokeshire where you might go in search of otters, but you are most likely to see them on this reserve.

country. Closer by, as the river emerges from the narrow gorge, slate waste from the quarries higher up the valley was dumped, although time and nature has now mellowed the appearance of the spoil with an over-growth of vegetation.

From the viewpoint follow the 'Gorge Trail' upstream, shortly passing the canoe centre and landing. A rougher path continues into the gorge beyond, energetically undulating and winding through the abandoned workings. Their harsh outlines are softened by trees and thick under-growth, where the dark, damp conditions have created a haven for lichen, ferns and mosses. Eventually the trail drops back to the riverbank and then shortly forks. Bear right, climbing steeply away from the water, meandering through more disused galleries before running more easily near the top of the gorge. Occasional breaks in the dense woodland give transient views across the valley, which by now has narrowed with sides so steep as to be almost sheer.

The gorge cuts through a fine deposit of slate, which was extensively quarried during the 19th century. The path through the ravine winds past many of the old workings. These prospered, in part, because the cut stone could be dropped straight onto waiting barges and taken downriver to Cardigan for onward export. The ugly moun-tains of sterile waste that are usually associated with such ventures are not immediately obvious here, as the rubbish was also loaded onto barges and dumped beside the Afon Teifi downstream. However, the practice contributed to the eventual closure of the quarries in 1938, for the river was eventually rendered unnavigable because of the accumulated debris.

Beyond a stile, the way continues to the left as a sunken, tree-lined track eventually leading to a farm. Ignore the gate ahead and instead cross a stile on the left back into the trees. Carry on through a conifer plantation, towards the far side of which the path turns to the right and shortly emerges over a stile facing two adjacent meadows. Go into that on the right and follow its left-hand hedge away, leaving at the end onto a narrow lane. A waymark guides you left, but then almost immediately, after a large house, turn right, dropping beside and then behind it to a bridge across a stream. Climb away to the left, coming out in Cilgerran on Church Street. The entrance to the castle lies along it off to the left, with the town just a little further on.

Cilgerran's first castle was thrown up by the Normans about 1092, a motte and bailey to support their advance onto the Pembrokeshire peninsula. It was soon extended, but times were troubled and during the next 130 years the fortress was twice taken by the Welsh. After William Marshal the Younger recovered the town in 1224 he had the castle rebuilt, and it is his work that we see today. But as the political climate settled during the later medieval period, the castle's strategic role diminished, and it gradually fell out

Below the gorge is an extensive riverside marsh

ST LLAWDDOG

Tradition holds that St Llawddog was one of 12 sons of the 6th-century King of Usk, and renounced his birthright in favour of a monastic life. He is credited with performing numerous miracles, and established a small hermitage monastery around which his cult grew. It is said that there has been a church here since that time, although the present edifice is largely Victorian, using slate from the local quarries. Interesting features include a plaque to Thomas Phaer who lived from 1510 to 1560. A man of many talents, he was a magistrate, writer, customs searcher and commissioner for piracy. Phaer also practised as a doctor and is remembered for pioneering work in paediatric medicine and a book on child care. William Logan has a spot in the graveyard; he founded the Geological Survey of Canada and is commemorated in the name of that country's highest mountain. Nearby is a splendid 'Ogham stone', one of several found in the area. A grave marker from around the 6th century for Trenegussus, son of Macutrenus (probably a local chieftain), it is interesting for an inscription carved in both Latin and Ogham script. Ogham was a form of writing used around the 4th century that consisted of a series of notches cut along the edge of a stone.

of use and became ruinous. This quality endeared it to Victorian artists, who flocked to capture its crumbling gothic walls on canvas. The restoration undertaken since it passed to the National Trust in 1938 may have robbed the castle of some of the Romantic mysticism portrayed by Turner and his contemporaries, but the work will ensure that its impressive defences survive for generations to come.

The way back follows Church Street in the opposite direction past the church. It deserves a look inside, but as the door is sometimes locked it might be worth first enquiring at the Camro Stores in the village, on the main road between Cilgerran school and the Square, where there is a key.

Fork right about 150yd past the entrance to the church, dropping to a bridge back over the stream. A path then climbs between cottages to a lane above, which you should cross to the left and follow a track away. Bend right as another track later joins, and then at a fork go right again through a barrier. Immediately beyond it, leave left at a waymark onto a woodland path, which subsequently widens to a track and leads to a gate. Do not go through, but instead pass to its right and follow a path at the fringe of the wood, eventually reaching a fork. Bear right to pass above a cottage, but at a waymark just a little further on, drop left onto a path signed 'Otter Trail'. Breaking from the trees, keep with the path at the edge of a meadow, now signed to the Visitor Centre and which returns past the main parking area.

The Ogham Stone in St Llawddog's Church graveyard

APPENDIX – USEFUL INFORMATION

Ordnance Survey maps

The following Ordnance Survey maps cover the area:
1:50,000 Landranger maps
Sheet 145 Cardigan and Mynydd Preseli
Sheet 157 St David's and Haverfordwest
Sheet 158 Tenby

1:25,000 Explorer maps
OL 35 North Pembrokeshire
OL 36 South Pembrokeshire

The spelling of Welsh names is not always consistent between different editions of the Ordnance Survey maps, and this book has adopted those appearing in the first Outdoor Leisure edition dated 1995.

Contact details

Pembrokeshire Coast National Park
Llanion Park, Pembroke Dock
SA72 6DY
☎ 0845 345 7275;
pcnp@pembrokeshirecoast.org.uk;
www.pembrokeshirecoast.org.uk

National Park Information Centres
Grove Car Park, St David's
☎ (01437) 720392
Bank Cottages, Long Street, Newport
☎ (01239) 820912

Pembrokeshire County Council
Pembrokeshire County Council,
County Hall, Pembrokeshire
Public Rights of Way issues
☎ (01437) 775109;
www.pembrokeshire.gov.uk

Tourist Information Centres
Harbour Car Park, Saundersfoot
☎ (01834) 813672

The Croft, Tenby
☎ (01834) 842404

The Commons Road, Pembroke
☎ (01646) 622388

Ferry Terminal, Pembroke Dock
☎ (01646) 622753

Kingsmoor Common, Carmarthen Road, Kilgetty
☎ (01834) 814161

94 Charles Street, Milford Haven
☎ (01646) 690866

The Old Bridge, Haverfordwest
☎ (01437) 763110

The Ocean Lab, The Parrog, Goodwick
☎ (01348) 872037

The Old Town Hall, The Square, Fishguard
☎ (01348) 873484

Theatr Mwldan, Cardigan
☎ (01239) 613230

Youth Hostels Association
Trevelyan House, Dimple Road, Matlock, Derbyshire DE4 3YH
☎ (01629) 592600;
customerservices@yha.org.uk;
www.yha.org.uk

Camping and Caravanning Club
Greenfields House, Westwood Way, Coventry CV4 8JH
☎ (024) 7647 5448;
www.campingandcaravanningclub.co.uk
Site booking ☎ 0870 243 3331

Transport
Pembrokeshire Greenways Coastal Bus Services
☎ (01437) 776313;
greenways@pembrokeshire.gov.uk;
www.pembrokeshiregreenways.co.uk

Traveline Cymru
☎ 0870 608 2 608;
www.traveline-cymru.org.uk

Local taxis
South Pembrokeshire
JB Taxi Hire
☎ (01646) 651789
Mobile: 07966 453649

Central Pembrokeshire
Stoddart's Taxis
☎ (01437) 781396
Mobile: 07855 462736/07968 336152

St David's peninsula
Frank's Cabs
☎ (01437) 721731
Mobile 07974 391522

North Pembrokeshire
Merv's Taxis
☎ (01348) 875129
Mobile 0783 6691222

Weather reports
Weathercall
☎ 0906 850 04 14

LISTING OF CICERONE GUIDES

The Great Glen Way
The Pentland Hills: A Walker's
   Guide
The Southern Upland Way
Ben Nevis and Glen Coe

IRELAND
The Mountains of Ireland
Irish Coastal Walks
The Irish Coast to Coast

INTERNATIONAL CYCLE GUIDES
The Way of St James – Le Puy to
   Santiago cyclist's guide
The Danube Cycle Way
Cycle Tours in Spain
Cycling the River Loire – The Way
   of St Martin
Cycle Touring in France
Cycling in the French Alps

WALKING AND TREKKING
IN THE ALPS
Tour of Monte Rosa
Walking in the Alps (all Alpine
   areas)
100 Hut Walks in the Alps
Chamonix to Zermatt
Tour of Mont Blanc
Alpine Ski Mountaineering
   Vol 1 Western Alps
Alpine Ski Mountaineering
   Vol 2 Eastern Alps
Snowshoeing: Techniques and
   Routes in the Western Alps
Alpine Points of View
Tour of the Matterhorn
Across the Eastern Alps: E5

FRANCE, BELGIUM AND
LUXEMBOURG
RLS (Robert Louis Stevenson) Trail
Walks in Volcano Country
French Rock
Walking the French Gorges
Rock Climbs Belgium &
   Luxembourg
Tour of the Oisans: GR54
Walking in the Tarentaise and
   Beaufortain Alps
Walking in the Haute Savoie, Vol 1
Walking in the Haute Savoie, Vol 2
Tour of the Vanoise
GR20 Corsica – The High Level
   Route
The Ecrins National Park
Walking the French Alps: GR5
Walking in the Cevennes
Vanoise Ski Touring
Walking in Provence
Walking on Corsica
Mont Blanc Walks
Walking in the Cathar region
   of south west France
Walking in the Dordogne
Trekking in the Vosges and Jura
The Cathar Way

PYRENEES AND FRANCE / SPAIN
Rock Climbs in the Pyrenees
Walks & Climbs in the Pyrenees
The GR10 Trail: Through the
   French Pyrenees

The Way of St James –
   Le Puy to the Pyrenees
The Way of St James –
   Pyrenees-Santiago-Finisterre
Through the Spanish Pyrenees GR11
The Pyrenees – World's Mountain
   Range Guide
The Pyrenean Haute Route
The Mountains of Andorra

SPAIN AND PORTUGAL
Picos de Europa – Walks & Climbs
The Mountains of Central Spain
Walking in Mallorca
Costa Blanca Walks Vol 1
Costa Blanca Walks Vol 2
Walking in Madeira
Via de la Plata (Seville To Santiago)
Walking in the Cordillera Cantabrica
Walking in the Canary Islands 1
   West
Walking in the Canary Islands 2 East
Walking in the Sierra Nevada
Walking in the Algarve
Trekking in Andalucia

SWITZERLAND
Walking in Ticino, Switzerland
Central Switzerland –
   A Walker's Guide
The Bernese Alps
Walking in the Valais
Alpine Pass Route
Walks in the Engadine, Switzerland
Tour of the Jungfrau Region

GERMANY AND AUSTRIA
Klettersteig Scrambles in
   Northern Limestone Alps
King Ludwig Way
Walking in the Salzkammergut
Walking in the Harz Mountains
Germany's Romantic Road
Mountain Walking in Austria
Walking the River Rhine Trail
Trekking in the Stubai Alps
Trekking in the Zillertal Alps
Walking in the Bavarian Alps

SCANDINAVIA
Walking In Norway
The Pilgrim Road to Nidaros
   (St Olav's Way)

EASTERN EUROPE
The High Tatras
The Mountains of Romania
Walking in Hungary
The Mountains of Montenegro

CROATIA AND SLOVENIA
Walks in the Julian Alps
Walking in Croatia

ITALY
Italian Rock
Walking in the Central Italian Alps
Central Apennines of Italy
Walking in Italy's Gran Paradiso
Long Distance Walks in Italy's Gran
   Paradiso
Walking in Sicily
Shorter Walks in the Dolomites
Treks in the Dolomites

Via Ferratas of the Italian
   Dolomites Vol 1
Via Ferratas of the Italian
   Dolomites Vol 2
Walking in the Dolomites
Walking in Tuscany
Trekking in the Apennines
Through the Italian Alps: the GTA

OTHER MEDITERRANEAN
COUNTRIES
The Mountains of Greece
Climbs & Treks in the Ala Dag
   (Turkey)
The Mountains of Turkey
Treks & Climbs Wadi Rum, Jordan
Jordan – Walks, Treks, Caves etc.
Crete – The White Mountains
Walking in Western Crete
Walking in Malta

AFRICA
Climbing in the Moroccan Anti-Atlas
Trekking in the Atlas Mountains
Kilimanjaro

NORTH AMERICA
The Grand Canyon &
   American South West
Walking in British Columbia
The John Muir Trail

SOUTH AMERICA
Aconcagua

HIMALAYAS – NEPAL, INDIA
Langtang, Gosainkund &
   Helambu: A Trekkers' Guide
Garhwal & Kumaon –
   A Trekkers' Guide
Kangchenjunga – A Trekkers' Guide
Manaslu – A Trekkers' Guide
Everest – A Trekkers' Guide
Annapurna – A Trekker's Guide
Bhutan – A Trekker's Guide
The Mount Kailash Trek

TECHNIQUES AND EDUCATION
The Adventure Alternative
Rope Techniques
Snow & Ice Techniques
Mountain Weather
Beyond Adventure
The Hillwalker's Manual
Outdoor Photography
The Hillwalker's Guide to
   Mountaineering
Map and Compass
Sport Climbing
Rock Climbing

MINI GUIDES
Avalanche!
Snow
Pocket First Aid and Wilderness
   Medicine
Navigation

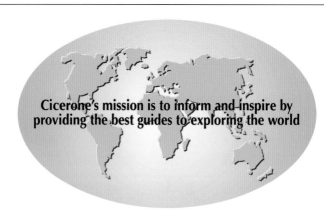

Cicerone's mission is to inform and inspire by providing the best guides to exploring the world

Since its foundation over 30 years ago, Cicerone has specialised in publishing guidebooks and has built a reputation for quality and reliability. It now publishes nearly 300 guides to the major destinations for outdoor enthusiasts, including Europe, UK and the rest of the world.

Written by leading and committed specialists, Cicerone guides are recognised as the most authoritative. They are full of information, maps and illustrations so that the user can plan and complete a successful and safe trip or expedition – be it a long face climb, a walk over Lakeland fells, an alpine traverse, a Himalayan trek or a ramble in the countryside.

With a thorough introduction to assist planning, clear diagrams, maps and colour photographs to illustrate the terrain and route, and accurate and detailed text, Cicerone guides are designed for ease of use and access to the information.

If the facts on the ground change, or there is any aspect of a guide that you think we can improve, we are always delighted to hear from you.

Cicerone Press
2 Police Square Milnthorpe Cumbria LA7 7PY
Tel:01539 562 069   Fax:01539 563 417
e-mail:info@cicerone.co.uk   web:www.cicerone.co.uk